Barriers or

Barriers or Benefits?

Regulation in Transatlantic Trade

David Vogel

Published for the
European Community Studies Association

Brookings Institution Press
Washington, D.C.

Barriers or Benefits? Regulation in Transatlantic Trade may be ordered from:
Brookings Institution Press
1775 Massachusetts Avenue N.W.
Washington, D.C. 20036
Tel: 1-800-275-1447
(202) 797-6258
Fax: (202) 797-6004

Library of Congress Cataloging-in-Publication data

Vogel, David, 1947–
    Barriers or benefits? : regulation in transatlantic trade / David Vogel.
        p.   cm.
    Includes bibliographical references and index.
    ISBN 0-8157-9075-9 (pbk. : alk. paper)
    1. Foreign trade regulation—United States.
    2. Environmental law—United States.   3. Foreign trade
regulation—European Union countries.   4. Environmental
law—European Union countries.   I. Title.
    K3943.V64   1997
    343.73'087—dc21   97-33926
                                                                          CIP

9 8 7 6 5 4 3 2 1

The paper used in this publication meets the minimum requirements of
the American National Standard for Information Sciences—Permanence
of Paper for Printed Library Materials, ANSI Z39.48-1984

Typeset in Palatino

Composition by Harlowe Typography, Inc.
Cottage City, Maryland

Printed by R. R. Donnelly and Sons Co.
Harrisonburg, Virginia

Foreword

DAVID VOGEL'S book on transatlantic regulatory cooperation is an important contribution to our understanding of the forces that animate politics in and set limits on the transatlantic marketplace. Using well-chosen instances of conflict and cooperation, he explains the sources and dimensions of problems with trade relations between the United States and the European Union. In light of their important implications for US-EU relations in both their transatlantic and global dimensions, Vogel's findings deserve the widest possible circulation. For that reason, the European Community Studies Association (ECSA-USA) is pleased to publish this policy monograph with the Brookings Institution.

Vogel's analysis also stands for a highly structured conversation among stakeholders affected by efforts to define and move the transatlantic trade agenda. By way of its US-EU Relations Project, ECSA desires to intervene in critical policy discussions so as to establish a mutually enriching channel of communication between the worlds of policymaking and academia. This volume is the third in the series that also includes Catherine Kelleher's *A New Security Order: The United States and the European Community in the 1990s* and Miles Kahler's *Regional Futures and Transatlantic Economic Relations*. For each monograph ECSA's Executive Committee defined a topic and selected an author. Then, armed with the author's early draft, the Association organized conversations on both sides of the Atlantic.

The 1997 US-EU Relations Project benefited especially from two institutional partnerships. Vogel's manuscript was the centerpiece of a Washington conference in January 1997 that was a collaborative effort with the American Institute for Contemporary German Studies (AICGS) at the Johns Hopkins University. In a remarkably productive session, sixty representatives of government agencies, business organizations, policy analysis institutes, and public interest groups were convened to respond to the manuscript. Exceeding the high expectations of the organizers, the assembled representatives went far beyond a critical review of the manuscript to engage in a fascinating discussion of their perceptions of operating at the frontiers of trade and investment liberalization. AICGS produced a conference report, *The Limits of Liberalization: Regulatory Cooperation and the New Transatlantic Agenda*, to document this process. ECSA is grateful to all the participants but especially those who provided statements to focus the conversation. This group includes Ambassador Ralph Ives (U.S. Trade Representative), Linda Horton (Food and Drug Administration), Frank Loy (League of Conservation Voters), Kenneth Feith (Environmental Protection Agency), Ted Austell (Trans-Atlantic Business Dialogue), Charles Stark (Department of Justice), William B. Garrison Jr. and Bradley D. Belt (both of the Center for Strategic and International Studies), Wolfgang Reinicke (Brookings Institution), Charles M. Ludolph (Department of Commerce), and Frances Irwin (World Resources Institute).

Two months later in Brussels, ECSA teamed up with the Trans-European Policy Studies Association under the able leadership of Wolfgang Wessels (University of Cologne) and Jacques Vandamme (Free University of Brussels). A similarly distinguished group from the European Commission, European Parliament, Trans-Atlantic Business Dialogue–Europe, European Trade Union Institute, European Partners for the Environment, and other organizations engaged in another discussion of regulatory cooperation. Special thanks go to Giandomenico Majone for contributing a thoughtful point of departure.

Little could have been accomplished without the active engagement of my colleagues serving on ECSA's 1997 US-EU Relations Project committee: Alberta Sbragia (University of Pittsburgh) and Leon Hurwitz (Cleveland State University). The committee defined the project format, marshaled the resources for the conferences, and organized the events that marked the way to this publication. In addition to the meetings in Washington and Brussels was the debut of the completed monograph at a plenary session of the ECSA biennial meeting, held this year in Seattle. All of us are indebted to administrative support from Bill Burros and his successor, Valerie Staats of ECSA, and to Wade Miller of AICGS.

ECSA gratefully acknowledges the assistance of the German Marshall Fund of the United States, the Directorate-General I of the European Commission, and the Boeing Company.

Carl Lankowski
American Institute for
Contemporary German Studies,
The Johns Hopkins University

Acknowledgments

I WOULD like to express my appreciation to Alberta Sbragia for encouraging me to pursue this project; the participants at the three workshops and conferences where I presented earlier drafts of this monograph for their helpful criticisms; and my research assistants, Tim Kessler, now on the faculty at the Claremont Colleges, and Eric Schulzke, a graduate student in the Department of Political Science at the University of California, Berkeley.

Thanks also to Martha Yager and James R. Schneider, who edited the manuscript; Carlotta Ribar, who proofread the pages; and Sherry L. Smith, who compiled the index.

To the memory of
Aaron Wildavsky

Contents

1   Introduction   1

2   Transatlantic Regulatory Cooperation   8

3   Consumer Protection   14

4   Environmental Protection   38

5   Conclusion   57

   Notes   67

   Index   75

1

Introduction

GOVERNMENT REGULATION has come to occupy an increasingly important place on the agenda of international relations. On the one hand, the role of environmental and consumer regulations as nontariff trade barriers has been the focus of a growing number of trade disputes, negotiations, and agreements. On the other hand, increased international regulatory cooperation has enabled nations to improve the effectiveness of their health, safety, and environmental regulations and has improved their ability to address common regulatory problems.

Because of their dominant position in the global economy, whenever the United States and the European Union (EU) agree on regulatory policies and procedures, many other nations are likely to adopt them as well. In effect, they become de facto global standards. Accordingly, a key conclusion of this essay is that the European Union and the United States need to become more active in promoting multilateral regulatory cooperation. At the same time, multilateral forums can facilitate the resolution of regulatory-related disputes between the United States and the EU.

Ironically, it is precisely because the EU and the United States have so much in common and are so economically interdependent that they have clashed so frequently over each other's regulatory policies. Because both are affluent, open societies whose citizens place a high value on consumer and environmental protection, each is continually enacting new regulations and strengthening existing ones. And because their trade is so exten-

1

sive to begin with, a significant portion of each partner's regulations affects the other's exports. This accounts for both the number of conflicts and the importance producers as well as citizens on both sides of the Atlantic have attached to them.

The extent and intensity of competition between European- and American-based firms has not led either political body to lower its regulatory standards to gain or maintain a competitive advantage. On the contrary, it is the steady strengthening of regulations on both sides of the Atlantic that has emerged as one of the most important sources of trade conflict between them. Likewise, regulatory cooperation between Europe and the United States has resulted in improving the effectiveness and efficiency of government regulation globally.

The European Union represents the world's most extensive effort to coordinate national regulatory standards. The progress the Europeans have made in creating a single market has significantly affected U.S.-EU trade relations. In some cases, the harmonization of regulatory standards within the EU has exacerbated trade tensions with the United States, while in others it has facilitated transatlantic regulatory cooperation. The experiences of the EU have also provided a model for other international efforts to strengthen regulatory cooperation, most notably those of the General Agreement on Tariffs and Trade/World Trade Organization (GATT/WTO).

This book explores the relationship between consumer and environmental regulation in U.S.-EU relations. It explains the dynamics of conflict and cooperation between the two entities in seven regulatory areas: food safety standards, labeling, and inspection; approval and inspection standards for pharmaceuticals; automotive fuel economy standards; chemical testing; animal protection; eco-labeling; and ozone depletion. These areas are not only individually important but illustrative of the pattern of transatlantic regulatory relations.

Six of the trade issues discussed here—bans on beef and dairy growth hormones, labeling of genetically engineered crops, meat inspection, the ban on leg-hold traps, and eco-labeling— involve U.S. complaints that actual or proposed EU regulations discriminate against American exports. Three other issues—fuel economy standards, the tuna embargo, and drug inspections—

stem from the EU's complaints about the obstacles to trade posed by American regulatory standards. Two disputes, the EU's challenges to American fuel economy standards and the American tuna embargo, have come before GATT dispute panels. The United States prevailed in the former case, the EU in the latter. A third dispute, which stems from an American complaint about the EU's beef hormone ban, is currently being adjudicated by the WTO. This study also examines three important instances of EU-U.S. regulatory cooperation. The two entities have worked closely on developing common testing standards for new chemicals, establishing more uniform standards for drug approval applications, and negotiating an international agreement to protect the ozone layer.

The pattern of U.S.-EU regulatory relations has important implications for the entire global economy. Together the United States and Western Europe account for more than one-third of world trade and approximately 55 percent of global GDP.[1] Not surprisingly, virtually all of their trade disputes over the alleged use of regulations as nontariff barriers have affected other countries as well. Other nations have intervened in a number of the disputes, usually supporting the complainant. Sometimes, as with the EU's beef hormone ban, the ban on leg-hold traps, and eco-labeling standards, this support has placed them on the side of the United States. In the case of the American tuna-dolphin ban, they have endorsed the position of the EU.

Policymakers' increasing attention to the role of government regulation in the global economy stems from the impact of these regulations on the international competitiveness of domestic firms and the effectiveness of government controls over business. Since World War II the scope of government intervention in national economies has expanded considerably. Along with the growth of the welfare state, this period witnessed a major expansion of government regulation of industry. Governments in advanced industrial societies as well as in developing ones enacted numerous rules, standards, and regulations to protect public health and maintain and improve environmental quality.

However, such regulations rarely affect all firms or industries equally because some producers find compliance easier or less expensive than others. Consequently, many regulations affect the competitive position of firms, offering advantages to some and handicapping others. Often these regulations, intentionally or inadvertently, favor domestic producers, thus functioning as nontariff trade barriers. Moreover, even regulations that do not directly impose greater costs on foreign producers may present obstacles to international commerce by increasing transaction costs. For example, importers may be required to submit their products to clinical tests or safety inspections that duplicate ones with which they have already complied at home. Such regulatory redundancy can significantly increase the costs of engaging in global trade.

When a country's regulations affect the competitive position, relative costs, or market share of foreign producers, the regulations cease being a country's own business and enter the sphere of international relations. The logic of trade liberalization has led governments to expand the scope of trade agreements beyond border controls such as tariffs and quotas to encompass a wide variety of regulatory policies, especially as border controls have declined in importance and regulatory policies have grown. Accordingly, many business-related policies that were formerly decided exclusively by national or local governments are now subject to international scrutiny and coordination. "Starting in the 1980s, the domestic structures of political economy have become major stakes in international trade negotiations."[2] By undermining national regulatory sovereignty, globalization has blurred the distinction between trade policy and health, safety, and environmental regulation.

International regulatory coordination cannot only promote trade liberalization but also can improve the effectiveness of national controls over domestic business. Many problems that national regulations address are either beyond the scope of the nation-state or can be controlled more effectively through international cooperation. Regulatory cooperation is necessary to reduce pollution and other environmental damage that crosses national boundaries or affects the global commons. International coordination may also be needed to enable nations to enact stricter national standards, because otherwise domestic producers with more expensive compliance costs than their trading partners would face a competitive disadvantage. Finally, a nation may reduce its own administrative burdens if its testing or inspection requirements are either identical or similar to those of its trading partners.

International agreements to reduce the use of regulations as nontariff barriers have primarily taken place under the auspices of the GATT/WTO. The Uruguay Round strengthened the Technical Barriers to Trade Agreement, also known as the Standards Code. This agreement limits the power of signatory nations to use regulations to protect domestic producers while permitting them to maintain or enact regulations necessary for legitimate public policy objectives. The Standards Code introduced the proportionality criterion into international trade law. This requires that national standards or technical barriers to trade not be "more trade-restrictive than necessary to fulfill a legitimate objective, taking into account the risks non-fulfillment would create."[3] At the same time, the code permits each national signatory to "maintain standards and technical regulations for the protection of human, animal, and plant life and health and of the environment."

The GATT/WTO itself has not attempted to establish either common or minimum regulatory standards. Its only authority is negative: it responds to complaints by telling nations if the burdens their regulations impose on international commerce are disproportionate to the objectives they are seeking to achieve or otherwise violate WTO rules on permissible trade restrictions. However, there is often a fine line between a legitimate health and safety regulation that is more difficult for a foreign producer to meet and a disguised form of protectionism. A number of the judgments of GATT dispute panels adjudicating national complaints about the use of regulations as nontariff barriers have proved highly controversial. Nongovernmental organizations (NGOs) have often sharply criticized the GATT/WTO for limiting the ability of governments to impose regulatory standards stricter than those of their trading partners.

The WTO has also sought to facilitate trade and minimize disputes by encouraging nations to adopt international standards. Thus the Uruguay Round agreement requires signatories to use international standards except when they would be "ineffective or inappropriate means for the fulfillment of the legitimate objective pursued."[4] There are various private, voluntary, international standards bodies, including the International Organization for Standardization, established in 1947, and several more standards bodies, such as the International Electrotechnical Commission, which deals with electrical and electronic goods, and the Codex Alimentarius Commission (the Codex Commission), which was established by two UN bodies to formulate international food product and processing standards. In the case of these food standards, the WTO agreement requires signatories to scientifically justify standards that differ from those of the Codex Commission if they discriminate against imports. Other international standards have been established under the auspices of the Organization for Economic Cooperation and Development (OECD) and the International Conference on Harmonization of Technical Requirements for the Registration of Pharmaceuticals for Human Use (ICH).

These standard-setting bodies have had their greatest success in establishing international standards, such as those for chemical and drug testing, that are primarily technical and benefit all producers equally. They have found it much more difficult to reach agreement on standards that confer significant competitive advantages or disadvantages, such as automotive fuel economy standards, or that raise significant public health and safety concerns, such as growth hormones or leg-hold traps. Still, uniform regulatory standards are not necessarily appropriate or desirable. There are many reasons nations may adopt distinctive standards, some of which, such as different income levels or distinctive tastes, preferences, or priorities, may be legitimate, while others, such as the capture of regulatory authorities by producer interests, are not. Once again, the distinction between the two is not always obvious.

To further encourage the use of international standards, the Uruguay Round agreement also introduced the concept of mutual recognition into international trade law. Like the doctrine of proportionality, this concept draws on EU jurisprudence. Mutual recognition became established in EU regulatory law through the decision of the European Court of Justice in *Cassis de Dijon* (1979), which required each member state to permit the sale of all goods lawfully for sale in any other member state unless it could demonstrate that its consumption adversely affected public health or safety. The WTO's Standards Code requires parties to give "positive consideration" to mutual recognition except when the regulations of the exporting country do not "adequately fulfill the objectives" of the importing country. In the case of food safety and processing standards, parties must be given the opportunity to "objectively demonstrate" the equivalence of their regulations to those of their trading partners.[5]

Although the GATT/WTO has been instrumental in reducing the use of regulations as nontariff trade barriers, other institutions have assisted in the international coordination of regulatory policy to strengthen regulatory effectiveness. The OECD has established a common set of testing methods for chemicals; data generated by the testing in a member country in accordance with OECD guidelines must be accepted by other member countries for the purposes of health, safety, and environmental assessment.[6] The recently established ICH, a more specialized international organization, has made substantial progress toward developing common registration requirements for ethical drugs in the United States, the European Union, and Japan.

Environmental treaties represent another important form of international regulatory cooperation. Agreements such as the Montreal Protocol and the Convention on International Trade in Endangered Species of Wild Fauna and Flora (CITES) have strengthened global environmental protection, in part by preventing less "green" countries from gaining a competitive advantage at the expense of their greener international competitors. These treaties, along with the work of the OECD and the ICH, demonstrate the critical role that international regulatory agreements can play in improving the effectiveness and efficiency of government regulation at the regional and national levels.

2

Transatlantic Regulatory Cooperation

A s EACH OTHER's largest investment partner and first or second most important trading partner, the EU and the United States have, in the words of former European Community Commissioner Christiance Scrivener, "the most important interdependent relationship in the world."[7] In 1993 EU-U.S. trade totaled 170 billion ecus, accounting for 7 percent of total world trade. However, "the distinguishing characteristic of the EU and U.S. economic relations is the mutual interlinkage through FDI [foreign direct investment]."[8] The two regions have considerable ownership interests in each other's markets: the EU is the source of more than half of all foreign investment in the United States, while more than 40 percent of U.S. overseas investments are in the EU.[9] The extent of this cross-national investment has affected the nature of EU-U.S. trade flows: approximately 40 percent of transatlantic trade in goods takes place within the same firm. This has given multinational European and American producers an important stake in maintaining well-functioning transatlantic ties. Not surprisingly, the transatlantic business community has emerged as a primary supporter of greater regulatory coordination between the United States and the EU.

The immediate impetus for promoting a transatlantic dialogue on regulatory standards and standard making was the European Community's 1992 internal market program. As the EC began to make progress in establishing EC-wide standards, Americans became concerned that the new regulations would be used to disadvantage American producers and products, in effect creating a "Fortress Europe." Fearing the loss of access to a market that accounts for one-fifth of its exports, the United States urged

8

the EC to permit American firms to participate in setting the standards and in certifying compliance with them.

Following negotiations between U.S. Secretary of Commerce Robert Mosbacher and EC Commission Vice President Martin Bangemann, the commission agreed in May 1989 to establish procedures for the participation of American firms in the EC's standards setting as well as to negotiate mutual recognition agreements (MRAs) for the inspection of product safety and quality. The MRAs would require the United States to allow non-U.S. entities and the EC to allow non-EC entities "to test products for conformity assessment purposes with a view of certifying them as being in compliance with local health, safety, environmental and more purely technical requirements."[10] Such an agreement on conformity assessment was regarded as extremely important because redundant testing and inspection requirements presented an obstacle to U.S.–EU trade at least as great as that posed by actual substantive differences in standards.

In the Transatlantic Declaration of 1990 the United States and the EU committed themselves to address and solve problems of common interest. A number of the subjects covered in this document involve regulatory matters, including "technical and non-tariff barriers to industrial and agricultural trade, services . . . transportation policy, standards, telecommunications and high technology."[11] One result of the declaration has been the issuing of annual reports in which each party sets forth its trade grievances against the other. These reports provide a comprehensive, constantly changing portrait of a critical dimension of EU-U.S. economic relations.[12]

The EC's 1992 report noted that divergent regulations among trading partners, each adopted for valid domestic reasons, resulted in significant barriers to trade. It urged that an "in-depth bilateral dialogue of the type envisaged by the Transatlantic Declaration" be held to reduce these barriers.[13] Dialogues were initiated for pharmaceutical regulation, food safety standards, the regulation of securities markets, air transport, and telecommunications. Aside from substantive policy differences and differences in regulatory styles, there was an important procedural obstacle to agreements between American federal regulatory agencies and the various directorates of the EU. None of them is legally authorized to enter into binding commitments, and any proposed regulatory changes must first go through each country's regulatory policymaking procedures. In the EU this generally involves the approval of a directive by the Council of Ministers; in the United States, regulations must be adopted according to the procedures of the Administrative Procedures Act.

As the regulatory competence of the EU has expanded, so have both formal and informal discussions between regulatory officials in Washington and Brussels. These officials now regularly monitor and exchange information about each other's proposals and policies, especially those likely to affect bilateral trade. This is one important way in which the centralization of regulatory policymaking in Europe has contributed to transatlantic regulatory cooperation. "Close cooperation of regulatory agencies . . . can help regulators better address their programmatic and enforcement responsibilities, improve relations with regulated industries, minimize unnecessary barriers to trade, and provide better health, safety, and environmental data to assist regulatory decisions."[14]

The EU has established the Unit for Regulatory Relations with the United States within the Directorate-General for External Relations. This unit has, in turn, established the EU-U.S. Interservice Group, consisting of representatives from most DGs. It is responsible not only for coordinating and overseeing regulatory cooperation with the United States, but also for promoting it. One of its first initiatives was to prepare a sector-by-sector inventory of issues subject to current or proposed bilateral cooperation to help resolve future trade disputes. There have also been ongoing bilateral negotiations between various DGs and their American counterparts to identify areas for additional cooperation with respect to food legislation, veterinary standards, pesticides, and biotechnology.

The United States and the EU have also established the Sub-Cabinet Group, headed by the director-general of DGI and the American undersecretary of state for economic affairs. In February 1994 the group issued a statement emphasizing the importance of cooperation on regulatory policymaking. The European Commission urged U.S. and EU regulatory officials to explore a wide variety of approaches for cooperating with one another, including working together on "technical issues for regulatory projects of joint interest, [making] greater use of each other's technical infrastructures, providing early warning of highly divergent or incompatible regulatory initiatives which may have trade implications, [and developing] mutual recognition schemes for conformity assessment, testing and certification."[15]

The United States has been particularly concerned about the trade impact of European standardization. The U.S. Department of Commerce recently estimated that "EU legislation covering regulated products will eventually be applicable to 50 percent of US exports to Europe," noting that this "evolving EU-wide legislative environment [has] caused concern to US exporters."[16] However, one of the difficulties in coordinating EU and American standards is that Europe relies much more heavily on international regulations, in part because it has employed them to help establish the single market. By contrast, American firms have historically relied less on international standards.

Promoting transatlantic regulatory cooperation has become an important priority for the private sector in both Europe and the United States. In 1995 a conference was held in Seville, Spain, under the auspices of the Transatlantic Business Dialogue (TABD), a business-led government-business initiative to lower trade and investment barriers across the Atlantic. Participants agreed to establish a Transatlantic Advisory Committee on Standards, Certification, and Regulatory Policy to work jointly toward a new regulatory model based on the principle "approved once, and accepted everywhere in the new Transatlantic Marketplace."[17]

A second conference held in 1996 in Chicago issued a declaration stating that "certain regulatory requirements, in particular duplicative testing and certification procedures and widely divergent technical regulations and standards, were no longer sustainable in terms of resources or results and were not suited to the realities of the global marketplace."[18] The participants urged officials on both sides of the Atlantic to make progress toward the principle of "one standard, one test, one time." In 1997 TABD issued a priorities paper noting that "several sectors consider completion of a Mutual Recognition Agreement (MRA) package to be a key demonstration of the effectiveness of the TABD process."[19]

In May 1997, after three years of intense negotiations, the United States and the EU announced a major agreement on conformity assessment. Each agreed to accept the other's inspection, testing, and certification standards for a number of products, including appliances, pharmaceuticals, and telecommunications equipment. This mutual recognition agreement means that "once a product receives the stamp of approval on one side of the Atlantic, it could be automatically sold on the other side as well."[20] The U.S. Commerce Department estimates that this agreement, which reduces one of the most important obstacles to transatlantic trade, could save American and European companies $172 million a year in legal and bureaucratic costs. The agreement covers $40 billion worth of goods, approximately one-fifth of total U.S.-EU trade.

A recent progress report on EC-U.S. relations published by DGI observed,

> Many problems faced by EC or US exporters/investors on each other's markets are not the deliberate result of protectionist inspired legislation but rather the unintended outcome of measures adopted for valid domestic reasons or of the differences which exist between the regulatory systems in the EC or the US.

The report added,

> The fact that the EC and the US share a fundamentally similar approach to the question of the market economy and that their citizens and consumers express similar concerns regarding the quality of products and health and environment protection, should however, make it feasible to encourage convergence in regulations and in the legislation on which they are based.[21]

The case studies of EU-U.S. regulatory relations discussed in this essay confirm the validity of the first part of this statement but not the second. It is true that regulatory-related trade conflicts across the Atlantic are not primarily due to the deliberate use of consumer or environmental regulations as trade barriers. Nonetheless, transatlantic differences in public values and in regulatory objectives and approaches remain large enough to make the goal of regulatory convergence elusive. Paradoxically, it is precisely because the United States and the member states of the EU are so politically and culturally similar that trade disputes between them are so common and intense: both are democratic, relatively open societies in which public policy is affected by public opinion and in which NGOs enjoy substantial political access and influence. The result is a fluid and constantly expanding regulatory agenda that has made the achievement of regulatory cooperation a moving target.

3

Consumer Protection

ONE of the most important areas of U.S.-EU regulatory relations involves health and safety standards for consumer products. This chapter examines the conflicts and cooperation over standards for food, agricultural products, and pharmaceuticals. These products illustrate two dynamics of regulatory cooperation. For food products, divergent national safety standards and inspection requirements have frequently represented an important barrier to international trade. Because many national food safety regulations and inspection standards benefit domestic producers and reflect strongly held, distinctive public preferences, efforts to reduce national differences in these regulatory policies often prove highly contentious. Accordingly, reducing the extent that food safety and inspection standards become trade barriers has been high on the agenda of the WTO, as well as the subject of extensive trade negotiations between the United States and the EU.

By contrast, distinctive and often redundant drug approval requirements have not been generally regarded as nontariff barriers, at least between the United States and the EU, primarily because they do not favor domestic producers. Whatever burdens they impose on foreign firms are equally onerous to domestic ones. Accordingly, international efforts to standardize drug approval procedures and requirements have been supported by virtually all pharmaceutical companies. By improving the effectiveness and efficiency of national drug approval policies, they have helped reduce the costs of and time for the approval of new drugs. The coordination of approval requirements and testing procedures has expedited government decisions on applications for new drugs while maintaining pubic health and safety. These negotiations, which are independent of trade institutions and negotiations, have been both remarkably cooperative and extremely productive.

Beef Hormones

One of the most bitter and protracted trade disputes between the EU and the United States stems from the divergence in standards for the sale of beef and beef products from animals that have been treated with growth hormones. Now lasting nearly two decades, this dispute demonstrates both the critical role of food safety standards as nontariff barriers and the difficulties in international regulatory harmonization.

The EU Hormone Ban

The dispute dates from 1980, when European newspapers reported that children in Italy were growing oversized genitals and breasts and attributed the condition to the fact that they had eaten veal treated with hormones. Large numbers of European consumers began to boycott veal.[22] Although the hormone used by the Italian cattle ranchers had already been banned throughout Europe and the United States, the scandal in Italy moved the use of growth hormones to a central place on the EC's regulatory agenda.

A debate in the European Parliament in July 1981 revealed a clear majority in favor of banning all five artificial and natural hormones then in use. However the Council of Ministers decided to sponsor a scientific inquiry to examine the safety of the hormones. The EC's investigation concluded that under appropriate conditions the three naturally occurring steroid hormones presented no health dangers. Because adequate data were lacking, it did not reach any conclusion on the two artificial hormones.

Despite this report, the EC found itself under growing pressure to ban the use of all growth-promoting hormones. The pressure came from two interrelated sources: the EC's commitment to the single market and European public opinion. Because hormone regulations had been neither harmonized nor made subject to mutual recognition, member states remained free to maintain their own standards. Six banned all five disputed substances, while the other half authorized the use of at least one. The continued disparity in national laws and the border checks that accompanied them presented a major obstacle to free trade in beef products within the EC.

In addition, European consumer and environmental groups had waged a vigorous campaign to prohibit growth hormones in animal production. In part because of their efforts, hormone use became a visible and emotional issue. The Bureau of European Consumers' Unions (BEUC), a coalition of national consumer unions, argued that the hormones created health problems for consumers and urged that they be banned. "The consumer organization's tough position could not be overlooked. It reflected a growing trend in Europe, fueled by the emergence of a strong ecology movement, in favor of 'natural' food products, even if this involved certain financial sacrifices." The BEUC further contended that growth-inducing hormones made little economic sense since the EC already had a large beef surplus. Calculating that half of the EC's 400,000 tons of stored beef was due to hormone-based production, the bureau concluded that "the only economic advantage of using hormones is to make profits for those who produce and use them."[23]

In 1985 the Council of Ministers agreed to harmonize hormone use throughout the EC. The Netherlands, Greece, and Italy favored a complete ban. They had already prohibited all growth hormones and wanted the EC to do the same to ensure a common market for meat as well as protect the economic interests of their inefficient beef producers. Although Germany did permit its farmers to use hormones, its strong domestic environmental, or "Green," movement persuaded it to join the antihormone camp. Great Britain and Ireland continued to favor the use of all five hormones. France and Denmark also opposed a general hormone ban.

In December 1985 the Council of Ministers voted to extend its hormone ban to the five substances omitted from its 1981 directive. As Frans Andriessen, the EC's agricultural commissioner explained, "Scientific advice is important, but it is not decisive. In public opinion, this is a very delicate issue that has to be dealt with in political terms."[24] Indeed, according to one observer, the decision to ban growth hormones marked "the first time the EC took into account the interests of consumers."[25] At the same time, the decision created a single market in beef throughout the EC. It thus simultaneously strengthened the single market *and* European regulatory standards.

International Impact

The hormone ban applied not only to beef and veal from cattle raised within the European Community, but to all beef and beef products imported into the (then) twelve member states. Most of the EC's major trading partners were relatively unaffected. Indeed Argentina, which produced large quantities of hormone-free beef, welcomed the ban as an opportunity to increase its exports to Europe. Canada protested the ban, but since its exports to the EC amounted to less than 0.02 percent of its total beef production, the economic impact of the directive was negligible.

The impact of the ban on American producers, however, was serious. The United States was the largest exporter of beef to the EC, shipping $120 million worth annually. And all five hormones are critical to American beef production. American meat exports to Europe consisted primarily of livers, kidneys, hearts, tongues, and other varietal meats. To supply the European market with such meats from cows that had not been treated with hormones, American producers would have had to alter the production of 7 million animals a year. Because each steer contained only about $25 worth of varietal meats, this was not economically feasible.

In December 1988, in an effort to diffuse criticism from the United States, the Council of Ministers voted to exempt meat intended for pet food from the ban. This accounted for about one-sixth of American meat exports to the Community, mostly to France. In January 1989 the ban was applied to all beef and veal marketed in the EC for human consumption, regardless of where it was produced.

The Basis of the Dispute

The United States objected to the EC's ban on hormone-treated beef on the grounds that because there was no scientific basis for the action, it represented an unnecessary obstacle to trade. The Americans noted that even the EC's own scientific advisory bodies had given three of the five hormones a clean bill of health. They further argued that rather than protecting the health of European consumers, the ban in fact put them at greater risk by encouraging an illegal hormone market in Europe.

The Europeans countered that the EC was within its rights to enact whatever regulations it deemed necessary to protect consumers regardless of the impact on trade, since "every country has the right under world trade rules to restrict imports for health reasons."[26] As French Minister of Foreign Affairs Edith Cresson said, "This isn't a way to avoid the importation of meat; it's a matter of health."[27] Jean François Boittin, France's permanent representative to the GATT, noted that the "ban simply represents the EC bowing to public pressure." He observed that although many scientific authorities had judged hormone-treated beef to be harmless, "the public is still opposed to the meat."[28] An EC official added, "Europe is democratic, it takes account of the needs of consumers, of political consensus within the Parliament and the vote of the Council."[29] In short, the ban was "no more a trade barrier than was Prohibition."[30]

In interviews with the American press Sir Roy Denman, the EC's ambassador to the United States, repeatedly raised the issue of American restrictions on unpasteurized cheese from Europe. For various health reasons the United States does not permit the sale of cheeses made from unpasteurized milk. It does make an exception for soft French cheeses such as brie, but only if they are baked first, which, Denman observed, "makes brie taste as much like real brie as apple juice tastes like a dry martini." Yet he claimed that the Europeans had never demanded a scientific inquiry into the dangers of eating brie from unpasteurized milk. Rather "they have accepted that Americans have expressed a democratic preference for hygiene over taste, however eccentric or unnecessary."[31]

The Dispute Escalates

The United States responded to the EC's hormone ban by imposing retaliatory tariffs of 100 percent on $100 million worth of EC agricultural exports to the United States. The amount represented the estimated value of America's loss of exports of beef and beef products to the EU. The Americans subsequently agreed to reduce their overall level of retaliation by the amount of hormone-free beef shipped to the EC from the United States. Shortly afterward, both beef and veal exports to the EC increased by $4 million, and the United States proportionately reduced its tariffs on the targeted agricultural products. However, although U.S. exports of beef and beef products to Europe increased to $34.3 million in 1994, the United States refused the EU's repeated requests for further reductions in retaliatory tariffs.

From the outset the American strategy was to refer the hormone dispute to international arbitration. In the fall of 1986 the Americans requested that the Codex Alimentarius Commission develop an international standard for hormone use. The commission's Committee on Residues of Veterinary Drugs in Food agreed with the United States that the EC ban represented "a classic example of a nontariff barrier with no scientific basis whatsoever."[32] Its Committee on Food Additives and Contaminants likewise gave the five growth hormones a clean bill of health. However, the Codex Commission itself, which consists of delegates from each of its member states and is the vehicle for government acceptance or nonacceptance of the recommendations of its technical committees, was reluctant to become embroiled in the conflict between the EC and the United States. At its biannual meeting in 1991 and again in 1993, it chose to ignore the recommendations of its own scientific bodies and either voted against or delayed issuing an international standard.

The United States also asked the Codex Commission to gather a group of technical experts to examine the scientific basis for the EC's ban, as provided for by the Standards Code, which had been enacted during the Tokyo Round. But the EC blocked the request on the grounds that the code only covered product standards and thus did not govern the use of hormones, which was a processing production method. The EC refused to accept the GATT's jurisdiction over the regulation, which meant that the United States had no legal grounds for requesting a dispute settlement panel.

The SPS Uruguay Round Agreement

In response to the impasse over the hormone ban, as well as its long-standing frustration about a number of other countries'—most notably Japan's—use of food safety regulations to restrict American exports, the United States proposed that the GATT be empowered to limit use of sanitary and phytosanitary (SPS) standards to keep out imports of "safe" food and agricultural products. As former U.S. Agriculture Secretary Clayton Yeutter put it, "We can't fool around for the next 25 years waiting for these international bodies to get standards done. . . . The GATT ought to have its own standards and then apply them."[33]

At the initiative of the United States, but with the support of other agricultural exporters, including Australia, New Zealand, and the EC itself, a limitation on the use of SPS regulations as trade barriers was incorporated into the Uruguay Round as part of a more general agreement on agricultural trade liberalization. Commonly referred to as the "Dunkel draft," after GATT Secretary General Arthur Dunkel, its purpose was to plug a major loophole in the Standards Code, namely the code's lack of an analytical framework for determining when a technical regulation that restricts trade is scientifically justified.

The Uruguay Round significantly strengthened the newly established WTO's oversight of national regulations and standards. First, it required all WTO signatories to abide by the new Agreement on Technical Barriers to Trade (the Standards Code), thus incorporating it into the WTO itself (compliance had formerly been voluntary). Second, it subjected technical barriers to trade to normal GATT dispute resolution procedures, which were also tightened. Third, it established a separate Agreement on Sanitary and Phytosanitary Measures (SPS), as a direct response to the hormone dispute, explicitly incorporating production and process methods within its scope.

The SPS Agreement represented an ambitious effort to establish international discipline over national and subnational food-related standards. It required nations to base their SPS measures on "international standards, guidelines and recommendations, where they exist."[34] The Committee on SPS Measures, established to implement the agreement, was instructed to work closely with the Codex Commission and rely on its scientific and technical advice. Measures that conform to Codex standards are presumed to be consistent with the rules of the WTO. If a nation wishes to impose stricter standards, it must demonstrate that they have a scientific foundation.

After the WTO was established, the Codex Commission again reviewed the issue of hormone use. At first it was stalemated, largely because of the EU's insistence that "standards cannot and should not be solely based on science and that consumer preferences should be taken into account."[35] However, in July 1995, "after extensive reviewing of scientific information had shown their safety to the consumer," the commission narrowly voted to approve the use of growth-promoting hormones in meat production.[36] Its decision was supported by a coalition of major agricultural exporters, including the United States, Australia, and New Zealand, as well as many developing countries.

The decision, though made by secret ballot, was denounced by EU Agricultural Commissioner Franz Fischler, who claimed that it had been made under pressure from the United States. He warned that it would "have no bearing on the EU's policy on hormones."[37] Later, the EU convened a conference of more than eighty leading scientists to try to break the impasse with the United States. The conference, however, endorsed a ten-year-old study, funded by the European Commission itself, which had found no evidence that the proper use of hormones posed a danger to human health.[38] But despite the lack of scientific evidence that the hormones posed a health threat, in January 1996 the European Commission reaffirmed its continuation of the ban on the grounds that "removal of the curb would alarm consumers and risk destabilizing the market."[39]

Because the SPS Agreement had brought the hormone ban under WTO jurisdiction, the United States lodged a formal complaint with the WTO. The United States claimed that the ban violated internationally recognized food processing standards, since beef produced with hormones had been certified as safe by the Codex Commission.[40] At the same time, to buttress its legal position with the WTO, it removed its retaliatory tariff on EU agricultural exports, over which the EU had filed its own complaint. The American complaint was backed by Australia,

New Zealand, and Canada, also major beef exporters. Three months later, EU agricultural ministers reaffirmed their support of the ban and approved measures strengthening its enforcement. Agricultural Commissioner Franz Fischler stated that the policy was not "simply a question of scientific evidence. It is also based on the need to prevent falls in meat consumption in the EU." He added, "The only course we can see is to defend the ban at the WTO."[41]

In May 1997 the WTO dispute panel issued a preliminary report finding the nine-year-old ban to be illegal on the grounds that it lacked adequate scientific justification. American officials were delighted with the ruling. One observed that the WTO had struck a blow against "a web of discriminatory practices . . . which are among the most pernicious barriers to trade in both the developed and developing world."[42] But even if the ruling is sustained on appeal, the EU is unlikely to permit the sale of beef produced with hormones. Popular suspicion of the use of chemical additives in food has remained strong in Europe; indeed recent reports in the European press have linked their use to a decline in male fertility rates. And the issue of meat safety has become even more salient since the outbreak of "mad cow disease."[43] European farmers worry that public uneasiness over beef hormones could destroy consumer confidence in beef just as it is starting to return after the mad cow crisis.

Under the rules established by the Uruguay Round, should the WTO decide in favor of the United States, the EU could still choose to maintain the ban, but would be required to compensate the United States for the losses sustained by American exporters, which the American National Cattlemen's Beef Association now estimates at $250 million a year. Although a spokesperson for the Cattlemen's Association stated that she was "hopeful that the US and the EU will sit down now and look at ways to get more US beef into Europe," the French agricultural minister stated that "France is entirely prepared to pay penalties if that is what is needed to prevent hormone-treated American meat from gaining entry to our territory."[44] For its part the Bureau of European Consumers' Unions strongly urged the EU to maintain the ban. It claimed, "Consumers don't want it, it brings them no benefits, and it could have disastrous consequences for consumer confidence in beef."[45]

The American Stake

At the time the ban went into effect, U.S. meat exports to the EC represented less than 5 percent of total American meat exports, which were then approximately $1.3 billion, 90 percent of which went to Japan. (Total annual American beef production amounted to $20 billion.) Moreover, the decline in meat exports to Europe was more than compensated by a surge in meat exports to Japan, Canada, and Mexico.[46] To put this dispute in perspective, the hormone ban affected less than 0.1 percent of total U.S.-EC trade. In short, by any objective measure, the European beef hormone ban was economically unimportant. Why then did the United States oppose it so vigorously?

Americans viewed the ban as linked to a much larger set of issues with very high stakes whose full import was likely to be extremely damaging. First, they feared that the European ban on beef hormones would encourage other EC regulatory requirements that would keep additional American products out of Europe. According to Food and Drug Commissioner Frank Young, the hormone ban suggested that as the EC moved to harmonize regulatory requirements to create a single European market, "it is not necessarily the most sensible rule that will prevail, but . . . the most stringent."[47] The ban thus seemed to confirm America's worst fears about the emergence of Fortress Europe, that the liberalization of Europe's internal market would be accompanied by an increase in external trade barriers.

Second, the United States was concerned that the ban would both legitimate and encourage its other trading partners to increase the use of health standards as nontariff barriers. For if the EC could successfully exclude an American agricultural product on what the Americans considered arbitrary grounds, might not America's other trading partners, especially Japan, be encouraged to seize upon this precedent to do likewise?[48] American Secretary of Agriculture Yeutter remarked, "If we permit [the hormone ban] to occur, in the [EC] or elsewhere, then we've opened up a gigantic loophole in the GATT which will result in major impediments to agricultural trade throughout the world for years to come."[49]

Finally, the hormone ban struck at a critical source of America's competitive advantage: its technically advanced agricultural production. If beef made from cows that had ingested growth hormones could be banned, what about processed food made with chemical additives, produce sprayed with post-harvest chemicals, or bioengineered food products—all of which regulatory authorities outside the United States might choose to ban following the lead and logic of the EC? Even more important, what would happen to the global market for all the advances in agricultural biotechnology on which American companies were currently working and in which the United States enjoyed a competitive advantage? It was thus not simply American farmers and food processors who stood to lose current and future markets, but also the American producers of agricultural technology.

Nor were these concerns merely academic. No sooner had the hormone ban been enacted than the Europeans introduced another restriction on an American agricultural technology: bovine somatotropin.

Bovine Somatotropin

Bovine somatotropin (BST) is a naturally occurring protein that can also be produced synthetically. When injected into cows, it increases milk production by 12 to 25 percent, about 500 pounds a year. In August 1989 the European Commission proposed to the Council of Ministers a moratorium on the use of BST. According to an EC official, the commission feared a "consumer backlash" if BST were approved. He said, "It's not easy to explain to customers that everything is all right when you are injecting drugs into cows."[50]

However, in contrast to the hormone ban, the EC's objection to BST was officially based on "social" rather than on health grounds. EC Agricultural Commissioner Ray MacSherry urged the European Commission to withhold approval of BST because it violated the EC's newly established "fourth criterion" for the approval of production-enhancing substances. In addition to the three criteria then current—safety, quality, and effectiveness—

the EC had decided to evaluate new agricultural technologies on the basis of "social and economic need." MacSherry claimed there was no "socio-economic need" for BST.[51] He expressed concern that the drug would lead to a "serious distortion of competition" because its benefits might not reach many small farmers. His position was supported by a number of organizations representing European dairy farmers.

The United States immediately voiced its strong opposition to an EC-wide ban. Indeed, according to one U.S. trade official, "This BST ban could potentially be far worse than the hormone ban. It might be used by a government to give itself license to prohibit the import of almost any product." U.S. Trade Representative Carla Hills stated that she was "troubled by a growing attitude in Europe and elsewhere that technological developments which encourage greater efficiency in agricultural production are socially undesirable."[52]

U.S. Agriculture Secretary Yeutter added that an EC ban on BST "would certainly contravene our mutual objective of achieving international harmonization in the sensitive area of food safety."[53] He claimed it "would also add fuel to the fires for those who wish to have public policy decisions made on the basis of emotion and political pressure." Another American official warned that the EC's decision to review a new biotechnology product on the basis of its "social and economic implications . . . could set a very dangerous precedent."

What concerned the United States was not the ban's impact on American exports of products from BST-treated dairy cows— in fact the EU has not excluded such products, whose volume is trivial in any event—but the loss of a significant market for sales of the hormone itself within Europe. Four U.S.-based firms— Monsanto, American Cyanamid, Eli Lilly, and Upjohn—had invested considerable sums in developing growth hormones not only for dairy cows but also for pigs, poultry, and sheep. A European ban on BST appeared to be the first step in closing off the global market, which industry officials have estimated at $500 million, with the EC projected to account for between one-third and one-half of this total.[54]

In September 1989 the EC adopted a proposal for a fifteen-month period to allow for scientific evaluations of BST and consultations with third-party countries. The following year the European Council requested member states to prohibit the administration of BST to dairy cows on their territory until the end of 1990. This ban was later extended, most recently in 1994 to the end of the decade. In January 1994 the U.S. Food and Drug Administration formally approved the use of BST, thus once again creating a divergence in food safety standards between the United States and the EU. At a meeting of the Codex Commission in June 1997, the EU successfully opposed a U.S. and Canadian effort to endorse the safety of BST, voting to defer a decision for two years to allow in-depth scientific research.[55] Thus this divergence in transatlantic regulatory standards is also likely to persist.

Genetically Engineered Crops

Differences have also emerged in EU and U.S. policies with respect to other bioengineered products. The United States has approved the sale of a number of genetically modified foods, but the EU has imposed far greater restrictions on the use of genetic engineering in agriculture.[56] As with the hormone and BST bans, these policies reflect differences in popular attitudes. A 1996 survey of European consumers reported that 85 percent would prefer not to eat genetically modified foods if given the choice.[57] Clearly, Europeans have been less willing than Americans to accept innovations in agricultural and food biotechnology.[58]

In October 1996, European food retailers and wholesalers called for genetically modified U.S. soybeans to be separated from ordinary ones (60 percent of all processed food sold in Europe contains soybeans).[59] About 2 percent of American soybeans had been altered by Monsanto to make them resistant to a herbicide that the firm also produces. Monsanto responded that separating the altered soybeans was both "impractical and unnecessary" because the product had been approved for sale by EU authorities in the spring of 1996.[60] Still, the German unit of Unilever, the Anglo-Dutch consumer products firm, canceled all orders for American soybeans, totaling 650,000 metric tons, unless they could be guaranteed to be free of genetically engineered soybeans. A number of other European food manufacturers also pledged to use only conventionally grown soya in their products.[61]

In the spring of 1997, several of Europe's largest food retailers from five countries, worried about consumer sqeamishness over biotechnology and seeking to restore confidence in food following the outbreak of mad cow disease, signed an open letter to the U.S. grain industry warning that several member states might require the complete segregation of genetically modified crops from traditional varieties unless American grain shippers agreed to identify which of their crops were genetically engineered. They warned, "Otherwise the 1996 harvest of genetically modified [crops] could indeed be the last to be welcomed in Europe."[62]

Their stance created considerable consternation among grain traders, because Europe annually imports $2.5 billion of American soybeans, and 15 percent of them are projected to come from genetically engineered plants. American grain producers, who export 25 percent of their soybean crop to the EU, argued that not only would it be prohibitively expensive to isolate genetically engineered soybeans and corn, but that there was no reason to do so since the crops from transgenic plants are nutritionally the same as those from traditional plants. A spokesperson for Cargill, the largest American grain exporter, stated that "the U.S. scientific and regulatory communities don't see the need for segregation [of genetically engineered crops]. And it just isn't practical."[63]

The European Parliament called for the suspension of sales of all genetically modified maize within the EU, a move criticized as irresponsible by the European Commission. Later the parliament approved legislation requiring the labeling of approximately 20 percent of genetically modified foods. This measure was welcomed by the European food industry but denounced by European environmentalists on the grounds that it did not adequately protect European consumers.[64] Although it was originally assumed that the rules would not be applied to products that had been already approved, such as Ciba's maize and Monsanto's genetically modified soya, the European Commission later stated that it would seek to extend them to these products as well. U.S. Secretary of Agriculture Dan Glickman declared, "We will not tolerate segregation [of genetically modified crops]," adding that "test after rigorous scientific test has proven these products to be safe. Sound science must trump over passion."[65] The Clinton administration announced that it would challenge before the WTO any attempts on the part of the EU to hinder imports of genetically engineered crops. The global stakes in these differences between European and American regulatory policies are considerable: the world market for genetically altered seeds is projected to reach an estimated $7 billion by 2005.[66]

In July 1997 the European Commission announced that it would issue rules requiring the labeling of all consumer foods that "may contain" genetically modified organisms (GMOs).[67] The Commission acted not only in response to public pressure, but also to maintain the single market, since Austria, Italy, and Luxembourg had already banned the import and sale of all GMOs, while France had refused to allow imports without a mandatory labeling requirement. The Commission's decision was greeted with relief by American and Canadian agricultural exporters, who had feared that the EU would require the segregation of GMOs throughout all stages of production and processing. The cost of complying with such a requirement would have effectively ended the use of GMOs in processed foods in Europe. It also was regarded as only mildly annoying by European and American food processors and packagers, who had feared the enactment of a much stricter labeling requirement.

The Commission's decision may actually facilitate both the sale and public acceptance of processed food made with GMOs. Not only does it override the ban enacted by the four member states, but the labeling requirement is so general that it is likely to cover the vast majority of grocery items sold in Europe. However, while temporarily avoiding a trade dispute with the United States and Canada, the Commission's decision is unlikely to appease European consumer and environmental activists, who remain highly critical of the application of biotechnology to agriculture. Regulations governing the sale and labeling of GMOs are thus likely to remain a source of trade friction.

Meat Inspection

Another point of contention has been the EU's reluctance to accept U.S. meat inspection standards. Unlike the disputes over hormones and genetically engineered crops, this conflict does not stem from differences in regulatory standards or popular preferences but from a lack of mutual recognition of inspection requirements. Indeed, one of the most persistent barriers to the creation of a single market for agricultural and veterinary products within Europe has been lack of confidence by many member states in the adequacy of one another's food inspection procedures.

The EC's Third Country Meat Directive (TCMD), originally enacted in 1972, has been amended on several occasions. Its purpose is to ensure that all meat sold in the EU is processed according to identical sanitary standards. This directive essentially applies the EU's harmonized meat inspection standards to meat produced outside the EU. It specifically requires that imported meat be produced in plants whose inspection systems and regulations are identical to those established by the EC for its member states. Inspectors were originally sent from Europe to certify individual plants. By the end of 1987, only 90 out of 1,400 American meat plants and cold storage facilities had been certified.

On July 14, 1987, the American Meat Industry Trade Policy Council filed a complaint with the U.S. Trade Representative (USTR) under section 301 of the Trade Act. Its complaint charged that the TCMD imposed an "unjustifiable and unreasonable restriction" on U.S. meat producers by limiting the number of plants certified to ship meat to the EC.[68] After the complaint the number of certified American plants increased slightly, reaching 125 by the end of 1989. However, this failed to satisfy either the American meat industry or American trade officials. Making matters worse, on October 25, 1990, the EC's Standing Veterinary Committee decided that American meat processing plant inspections did not meet EC veterinary standards because the U.S. inspections lacked "adequate hygiene and veterinary controls as well as postmortem inspections of animal carcasses."[69]

The EC informed the U.S. secretary of agriculture that if inspections on EC-approved third-country (non-EC) slaughterhouses were not improved, it would begin to restrict American meat exports. The next month, the EC announced that it would no longer allow American-made pork products to enter Europe.

A year later, this ban was extended to beef imports as well. The economic significance of this restriction was modest: before the ban, U.S. pork exports to the EC had averaged only $10 million a year, and beef exports had already been substantially curtailed by the hormone ban.

Nonetheless, the EC's enforcement of the TCMD angered American industry and government officials. The United States argued that while its veterinary inspection standards were not identical to those of the EC, they were equivalent and thus the ban constituted a nontariff barrier.[70] American industry officials also accused the EC of discriminating against American meat products, since a number of food processing plants within the EC also were not in compliance with the veterinary inspection directives. The EC, however, continued to insist that American standards be identical to those required by Brussels.

In November 1990, American beef and pork producers filed a section 301 complaint with the USTR. The USTR accepted the complaint but sought to negotiate the dispute. The negotiations achieved only modest results: the EC agreed to recertify four plants and to consider the recertification of others pending on-site inspections. In 1992 some progress was made. The United States and the EU adopted the findings of a joint U.S.-EU veterinary group. The EU agreed to amend the Meat Directive to provide for recognition of equivalent inspection systems in third countries by January 1995. But this target date was not met. Following the Uruguay Round agreement, the European Commission entered into negotiations with the United States to establish a framework agreement to permit recognition of equivalence between U.S. and EU standards. After nearly three years of negotiations, agreement was finally reached on mutual acceptance of inspection standards for a number of animal products.

In the spring of 1997, however, trade friction heated up again. The EU introduced rules requiring compliance with its hygiene standards by all exporters from nations with which it had not yet reached mutual recognition agreements for the exporters' products.[71] This meant that U.S. producers would no longer be allowed to export agricultural products for which no agreement on veterinary equivalence had been reached with the EU. The rule affected American exports of red meat, poultry, eggs, dairy products, and fish worth more than $125 million a year. In response, the U.S. announced that it would retaliate by blocking EU meat and poultry exports worth $300 million a year.

After intensive negotiations, a transatlantic trade war over food was narrowly averted when the two sides agreed to accept each other's testing and inspection systems and procedures. This agreement, which covered more than $1.5 billion worth of trade in agricultural products, constituted a significant step toward resolving this long-standing source of trade friction. But the two sides were unable to reach agreement on poultry inspection standards because the EU refused to accept the American practice of decontaminating poultry with chlorine rinses. The Americans claimed that this practice is safer than the processes used by the EU, and American poultry producers accused the EU of using the inspection standards as a "blatant attempt to restrict competition from US poultry companies."[72] The United States in turn decertified all EU poultry establishments, thus effectively ending U.S.-EU trade in this product. The EU contended that the American action was unjustified because European producers had clearly indicated their willingness to comply with American requirements. Still, this impasse affects only a relatively small amount of trade: in 1996, American exports of poultry to the EU amounted to $50 million while the EU exported only $1 million worth of chicken pâté to the United States.

Pharmaceutical Products

Until recently, the EU had made considerably slower progress in harmonizing approval procedures for legal drugs than for many other products, including food.[73] The reluctance of the member states to surrender national control over drug approval policies and procedures was due not only to their distinctive regulatory approaches and cultural and social values, but also to the close ties between drug approval policies and national health care policies. Approximately half the drug industry's revenues in Europe come from national governments. In addition to controlling new product registration, member states also control drug prices and subsidize development costs, making this industry among Europe's most extensively and closely regulated.

After ratification of the Maastricht Treaty on the European Union in 1992, the EU established a new regulatory institution, the European Medicines Evaluation Agency (EMEA), and two new procedures for drug approval, one based on harmonization and the other on mutual recognition. Its objective was to create a single market for pharmaceutical products within Europe by the end of the decade. Thus, instead of filing fifteen separate applications, most with different requirements, drug firms can file only one. In October 1995 the first pan-European drug was approved: Gonal-F, a fertility treatment. To date, thirty-three have been given marketing approval throughout the EU.[74] This development, in turn, has made possible for the first time the coordination of drug approval requirements at the international level.

As for U.S. practices, before the mid-1980s cooperation between the U.S. Food and Drug Administration and its counterparts in other nations was limited. The FDA had entered into an agreement defining good manufacturing practices with Switzerland, Sweden, Canada, and Japan and had also signed an agreement establishing good laboratory practices with Canada and seven European countries.[75] However the United States required that clinical testing for all drugs, domestic or imported, be performed in the United States. This forced exporters to duplicate costly tests and restructure trials to conform to American laboratory standards. "This policy seems to have had a significant effect in delaying the introduction of foreign-discovered drugs into the United States—even those foreign drugs that represented significant advances." But the FDA regarded foreign clinical data as "too precarious" to serve as the basis for a marketing approval decision.[76]

The FDA had long been criticized for the "drug lag," the length of time it took before a drug approved in a European country became available in the United States. During the mid-1980s AIDS activists sharply criticized the agency for its delays in approving drugs that might be effective against the deadly virus.[77] In part as a response to these pressures, the FDA adopted guidelines allowing research conducted outside the United States to be incorporated into both animal and clinical trial applications.[78]

In 1990 the United States and the European Commission completed a memorandum of understanding that standardized good
drug manufacturing and laboratory practices. The next year, as
part of a more comprehensive regulatory reform package, U.S.
Health and Human Services Secretary Louis W. Sullivan announced the FDA's interest in harmonizing American testing
standards with those of other industrialized nations. Sullivan
expressed the hope that harmonization would lead to the "development of common testing procedures [that] would reduce
. . . duplication [of tests] and speed the development of drugs
worldwide."[79] Four days later the President's Council on Competitiveness called for "reciprocity agreements," or mutual recognition of drug approval, to be "negotiated on a country-by-
country basis."[80]

The International Conference on Harmonization

The International Conference on Harmonization of Technical
Requirements for the Registration of Pharmaceuticals for Human
Use (ICH) grew out of meetings among regulatory officials from
Europe, the United States, and Japan and the International Federation of Pharmaceutical Manufacturers Association. Its first
session took place in Brussels in 1991, shortly after the EC's
Council of Ministers began drafting the Maastricht Treaty. The
renewed commitment of the EC/EU to establish regional regulatory standards made it much more practical to seek agreement
on global ones. ICH participants included officials from the U.S.
FDA, the EU's Committee for the Proprietary Medicinal Products, and the Japanese Ministry of Health and Welfare as well as
representatives from pharmaceutical companies in the EU, the
United States, and Japan. These three markets account for 75
percent of the world's production of medicines and 90 percent
of global pharmaceutical research and development.[81]

More than 1,000 participants attended the first ICH conference. In addition to establishing a process of negotiated rule
making to harmonize regulatory guidelines, the conference approved a "minimum data blueprint" guideline, later incorporated into U.S., EU, and Japanese law.[82] The blueprint defines
data collection conditions acceptable in the three markets, thus

allowing a firm to file the same data package in each. Although the data submitted are still evaluated by national officials who may still demand information beyond the scope of the minimum data blueprint, the guideline eliminated the need for costly and repetitive tests.

The guideline also standardized long-term toxicity tests, limiting repeated dose toxicity studies to six months.[83] This was expected to "cut industry's costs by a total of $100 million annually—and save the lives of 35,000 laboratory animals, itself an increasingly important consideration."[84] According to one estimate, the minimum data blueprint's elimination of duplicate testing will save the EU up to 100,000 ecus for each new medicinal product, and reducing long-term toxicity tests from one year to six months will save as much as 500,000 ecus for each new substance.[85] The most important outcome of the 1991 conference was, however, a political one: it committed the "Big Three" regulatory agencies—the EMEA, FDA, and Japan's MHW—to the principle of harmonization.[86]

A second ICH conference was held in October 1993 in Orlando, Florida. In his keynote address to the conference's 1,600 participants, FDA Commissioner David Kessler stated, "Science-driven harmonization can curtail duplication, and thereby significantly reduce the cost of new drug development—not just in dollars spent by the industry but in the risk taken by patients, in the experimentation with laboratory animals, and in the regulatory efforts of our governments." He added, "It has the potential for a major breakthrough in the drug approval process by making a common registration package a realistic possibility."[87] The Orlando conference established common procedures for animal-based experiments to detect toxicity in reproductive systems and established common definitions and standards for clinical safety data management.[88]

A third session, attended by 2,400 delegates from pharmaceutical firms and forty governments, took place in Yokohama, Japan, in November 1995. It produced agreements on uniform guidelines for the clinical testing of new drugs and good clinical practice. These agreements are intended to facilitate the mutual acceptance of data on clinical trials, thus significantly reducing the costs of drug development. ICH3 also agreed on a program to complete the development of fifty common guidelines on the steps necessary to demonstrate the safety, quality, and efficacy of new medicines. One ICH group is working on harmonizing the medical technology used by regulatory agencies and developing electronic data transmission standards. Agreement on these standards will eventually enable a company to electronically submit the same dossier or application to the FDA, EMEA, and MHW. At the closing plenary session of the conference, Roger Williams, deputy director of the FDA's Science and Medical Affairs Center for Drug Evaluation and Research, stated, "We've just stepped up close to the realization of a dream. We can say it's a global dossier, which is available through any country in the world, or is acceptable to any regulatory authority in the world."[89]

Nineteen guidelines have been formally approved by conference participants, four of which have been enacted into law in Europe, the United States, and Japan, while an additional thirty-eight are being developed.[90] What is especially significant is that many firms in the United States, Japan, and Europe have already adopted the first eleven guidelines.[91] The world's twenty-five largest drug firms have adopted nearly all of them.[92] The ICH meetings have also improved communication and trust among regulators in different regions and fostered the establishment of more sophisticated and comprehensive mechanisms for data exchange, including an experimental effort to share data on floppy disks and through the Internet regarding the side effects of previously approved drugs.[93] The ICH's long-term objective is to adopt sufficient guidelines to create a core dossier for each drug that would be acceptable to regulatory bodies in the United States, Europe, and Japan.

The ICH has had a strong impact on Japanese testing procedures and requirements, which have generally provided far less public protection than those in the United States and Europe. Moreover, each successive meeting has been attended by delegates from additional countries. In light of the dominance of the global pharmaceutical industry by U.S., EU, and Japanese firms, it is likely that ICH guidelines will be also adopted by many other countries. For its part, the World Health Organization has begun to encourage developing countries to enact them. As one American regulatory official said, "ICH has been far more successful than anyone anticipated."[94]

Not surprisingly, it is the EU that has made the most progress in adopting ICH standards and guidelines. Most guidelines "largely overlap with current EC legislation, so the ICH guidelines do not imply any major changes in the EEC acceptance policy for pharmaceutical products."[95] The Europeans' broad experience in harmonizing regulations within the EU has enabled them to be the leader in promoting international regulatory cooperation. At the same time, the progress made by the ICH in standardizing testing requirements has contributed to the harmonization of drug approval standards and procedures within the EU.

For its part, the FDA has become increasingly willing to work with foreign regulatory agencies. Between 1992 and 1995 it published four rules in the *Federal Register* that progressively eliminated its barriers to sharing information with its foreign counterparts.[96] The agency has also formed internal groups that mirror those established by the ICH's steering committee, and their recommendations have reduced the number of overlapping requirements imposed on firms seeking American marketing approval.[97] At the same time, thanks in large measure to legislation enacted in 1992 permitting the FDA to charge drug companies user fees, the drug lag between Europe and the United States has virtually disappeared, thus facilitating further transatlantic regulatory cooperation.[98]

A number of the EMEA's criteria for efficacy and effectiveness, as well as its requirements for clinical review and scientific vigor, are sufficiently similar to those of the FDA to permit the agencies to rely more on each other's data.[99] Thus in the case of drug regulation, in contrast to food safety and inspection standards, the creation of a single market in Europe has facilitated U.S. and EU regulatory cooperation. Moreover, the work of the ICH has been paralleled by continuing bilateral meetings between the FDA and the European Commission to explore additional ways of harmonizing their regulatory policies and procedures. "The long-term goal for Brussels is mutual recognition of all new-drug registrations," a goal shared by pharmaceutical firms on both sides of the Atlantic.[100] Although achieving this goal is unlikely in the near future, a common standard for a drug approval application between Europe and the United States is now a strong possibility, thanks to the formation of the EMEA and the work of the ICH. The result will make it easier for European and American companies to market identical or similar medical products on both sides of the Atlantic at roughly the same time and will significantly lower drug testing and approval costs.

Inspection

Restrictions on trade in the bulk ingredients used to manufacture pharmaceuticals have been an important source of contention between the EU and the United States. As with meat products, this dispute has hinged on the lack of mutual acceptance of each other's inspection systems. But this time it has been the United States that has refused to accept European inspections.

Underlying this dispute is a history of American doubts about the adequacy of foreign inspection standards. As a result the FDA has frequently undertaken its own on-site inspections rather than rely on European government inspectors. Between 1977 and 1991 the FDA audited sixty-six non-U.S. sites in fifteen countries, including a number in Europe.[101] It found many shortcomings, among them unavailable or inadequate records and failure to adhere to protocol.

As part of negotiations on a mutual recognition agreement to reduce regulatory barriers to trade, the EU proposed mutual recognition of official plant inspections. One difficulty was to decide how an agreement on inspection of joint manufacturing practices would work.[102] The Americans wanted to be able to evaluate the inspection reports of EU authorities and draw their own conclusions. The EU insisted that the FDA rely on the conclusions of EU inspections. The United States also expressed concern about the inability of Brussels to enforce any U.S.-EU agreement on inspection standards because each member state operated its own inspection process. This impasse was finally resolved in June 1997 when, as part of the mutual recognition agreement reached between the EU and the United States, the FDA retained its legal right to certify all pharmaceuticals produced in Europe and exported to the United States but agreed in practice to accept European inspection standards.

4

Environmental Protection

ENVIRONMENTAL PROTECTION policies represent another important dimension of U.S.-EU regulatory relations. This chapter begins by discussing three cases of EU-U.S. trade conflicts over environmental regulations, two of which are ongoing. It then explores U.S.-EU international regulatory cooperation on environmental issues.

CAFE and Automobile Taxes

The most important environmentally related trade dispute between the EU and the United States occurred in 1993 when the EU requested the convening of a dispute settlement panel to rule on the GATT-consistency of American corporate average fuel economy (CAFE) standards and two automobile taxes. The EU complained that all three burdens fell disproportionately on European automakers. Although European cars accounted for only 4 percent of American sales in 1991, they contributed 88 percent of the revenues collected by the two taxes and CAFE penalties, a total of $494 million.[103]

The purpose of the CAFE standards, established in 1975 and tightened in 1980, is to promote fuel efficiency. They are based on the miles per gallon achieved by a sales-weighted average of all vehicles produced by a manufacturer. If a manufacturer's vehicles fall below this standard, which has been set at 27.6 miles per gallon since 1990, it faces a penalty of $5.00 for every tenth of a mile per gallon that its vehicles fall short, multiplied by the number of vehicles the manufacturer sold in the United States.

Although this penalty applies equally to all car manufacturers, in the two decades since the standards were introduced it has been paid exclusively by European makers of limited-line premium cars. Because all American automobile firms make a full line of cars, they have avoided the tax on their less fuel-efficient luxury cars by averaging the fuel economies of their entire fleet. Japanese automakers have avoided the tax because they make mostly small fuel-efficient vehicles. According to A. B. Shuman, public relations manager for Mercedes-Benz of North America, CAFE rules "are really made for the Big Three. The problem for Europeans is that . . . they don't have little cars to balance out the higher-consumption cars."[104] Accordingly, the EC claimed that because CAFE penalties fell only on imported cars, they violated the GATT's national treatment provision.

CAFE penalties have been substantial. In 1983 Jaguar missed the CAFE standard by 7 miles per gallon and was required to pay a penalty of $350 for each car it sold.[105] Between 1985 and 1989 Jaguar paid CAFE penalties totaling $27 million, BMW paid $32 million, and Mercedes-Benz paid $85 million.[106] Only one major high-end European car exporter, Saab-Scania, met the 1989 CAFE standards, and that was because it sold only cars with four-cylinder engines. Thanks to CAFE penalties, American consumers have recently been required to pay an additional $1,800 for a Jaguar XJ-S V12 and $1,500 for the Mercedes 560SEC sport coupe.

The EC's complaint also challenged the GATT consistency of the two other vehicle taxes it claimed discriminated against European automobile exports. One of these is the "gas-guzzler" tax levied on passenger vehicles whose fuel economy is less than 22.3 miles per gallon. In contrast to the CAFE penalty, this tax is based on the fuel economy of particular models rather than on the corporate average. Established in 1978, it was doubled in 1991 and now begins at $1,000 per vehicle. The EC argued that the gas-guzzler tax was not only discriminatory but was not based on objective or reasonable criteria.

The other tax challenged by the EU applied to luxury cars. In 1985, in order to raise additional revenue, the United States imposed an excise tax on cars costing more $16,000 that were bought for business use. In 1991 the tax was amended to apply to all cars costing more than $32,000. The EU claimed that this

$30,000 cutoff was capricious and discriminatory because in 1990, the year the tax was introduced as part of the budget reconciliation bill, more than 80 percent of the vehicles subject to it were imports.[107]

The cumulative economic impact of the three taxes and penalties was significant. For example, in 1992 Mercedes-Benz paid a total of $216 million in fines and taxes, about $3,500 for each car it sold in the United States. The EC charged that all three measures were protectionist because they "individually and collectively [had] a discriminatory incidence on car imports."[108]

Although the EC's complaint addressed all three American rules, its challenge to CAFE attracted the most attention. American environmental and consumer groups have always strongly supported CAFE, defending it against critics and frequently supporting efforts to strengthen it.[109] The American environmental organization Friends of the Earth sharply criticized the EC's decision to file a complaint, claiming that "the EC cannot claim to be concerned about the development of the trade and environment debate if it persists in attempting to define . . . whether or not the environmental laws of another country are simply disguised trade barriers."[110] Trade analysts in the United States expressed concern that a GATT ruling against the United States would add to the GATT's reputation as anti-environment, since two of the three laws it had challenged were designed to encourage conservation. This would have made it more difficult to secure congressional approval of a completed Uruguay Round agreement. One environmental trade expert predicted, "The CAFE standards are so central to [U.S. clean air safeguards] that it would do the GATT a lot of harm if it does rule against the United States."[111]

In the fall of 1994 the GATT dispute panel found all three taxes to be GATT consistent. The panel concurred with the EU's claim that fuel efficiency could be achieved in less trade-restrictive ways (by increasing gasoline taxes, for example), but it declined to hold the United States to a "least trade restrictive" standard. Rather, it concluded that the United States needed only to demonstrate that its regulation achieved a legitimate environmental objective, a category that included fuel conservation. The panel also upheld the GATT consistency of both the gas-guzzler and luxury taxes because they were levied on products rather than companies.

The United States was extremely pleased with the ruling. According to U.S. Trade Representative Micky Kantor, "The panel has emphatically rejected the Europeans' claim that trade-neutral legislation intended to further energy conservation goals and protect the environment could be attacked because Chrysler, Ford and GM invested and complied with the law while Mercedes and BMW chose not to and had to pay penalties."[112] The panel did, however, rule that the CAFE provision requiring companies to meet fuel economy averages for both their domestic and imported cars (the so-called separate fleet accounting rules) was GATT inconsistent because it treated similar products differently on the basis of where they were manufactured. But the United States refused to change this provision, arguing that it had no adverse impact on European companies because all their cars were imported.

The EU sharply criticized the American refusal. As one EU official declared, "We object to the fact that the United States appears unwilling to change the CAFE law. . . . Such a posture by the United States does not bode well for the future of the multilateral trade system of the World Trade Organization."[113] The EU officially remarked, in language reminiscent of the slippery-slope imagery that characterized the U.S. response to the EC's ban on beef hormones, that the GATT panel report, "constitutes a backward step . . . that risks opening the door for inventive tax and regulatory authorities to discriminate against imported products."[114]

Wildlife Conservation

The imposition of import restrictions that affect conservation practices outside their borders has been another important source of contention between the EU and the United States. The U.S. has restricted imports of tuna from Europe; the EU has sought to ban fur imports from the United States.

Tuna and Dolphin

During the late 1960s, marine mammal protection emerged as an important political issue in the United States. Congress responded in 1972 by enacting the Marine Mammal Protection Act. To protect dolphins in the eastern tropical Pacific from being killed by tuna fishermen, the MMPA established a dolphin kill quota for American vessels. Although the legislation and the subsequent amendments to it established similar requirements for foreign fishing vessels whose tuna was exported to the United States, this provision was not enforced.

In 1990 the Earth Island Institute, a California-based nongovernmental organization, took the Department of Commerce to court to demand that the MMPA's restrictions on tuna imports be enforced. The suit was successful. The U.S. district court ordered the Commerce Department to ban imports of tuna from Mexico and Venezuela because the fishing practices of their fleets violated American dolphin protection standards. A subsequent court decision ordered the department to impose a secondary or intermediate embargo as well: tuna imports were banned from nations that continued to purchase tuna from the countries subject to the primary or direct embargo. This list initially included Japan, Costa Rica, Panama, and two EC member states, France and Italy. It was later expanded to include twenty more countries.

Mexico immediately filed a complaint with the GATT. It claimed that GATT rules prohibit a nation from restricting the import of a product on the basis of how it is produced. Mexico's complaint was supported by the EC and a number of other nations; the EC reiterated its long-standing objections to American unilateralism in pursuit of global environmental objectives.[115]

In April 1991 a GATT dispute panel ruled that the tuna embargo violated America's GATT obligations, since, according to the trade agreement's "national treatment" provision (article III), imports could be restricted only on the basis of characteristics of the product itself, provided similar restrictions are imposed on domestically produced products. The panel found that the agreement did not permit a signatory nation to "restrict imports of a product merely because [the product] originates from a country with environmental policies different from its own."[116] The ruling outraged American environmentalists, who accused the GATT of undermining American conservation policies in order to promote free trade. It was, however, hailed by the EC and almost every other U.S. trading partner, many of whom resented America's frequent use of unilateral trade sanctions to influence the conservation practices of its trading partners.

The EC argued that "what had started as a dispute between two parties was now of interest to us all." It demanded that the GATT Council hold a full debate on the ruling in order to correct the false "impression in some quarters that the [ruling] had placed environmental and trade issues on a collision course."[117] Frustrated that the panel report enjoyed no legal standing because the United States refused to accept it, the EU, acting on behalf of Spain and Italy, two member states subject to the American secondary embargo, requested that a second panel deliberate on the tuna ban.

In its brief, the EC stated that "while it agrees with the environmental goal being pursued by the US, it objects to the United States imposing its laws on the rest of the world."[118] (In fact, the EC had recently imposed dolphin protection standards similar to those of the United States on its fishing vessels, but not on imported tuna.) The EC also claimed to have suffered substantial economic injury because tuna that otherwise would have been sold in the United States was flooding the world market and lowering global tuna prices. The United States responded that far from being protectionist, it had imposed even more stringent requirements on its own fishing fleets. It further argued that "there is nothing in the General Agreement that distinguishes between 'unilateral' measures and other types of measures." In fact, "the vast majority of measures taken by sovereign nations in all fields of activity are unilateral."[119]

In June 1994 a GATT dispute panel found the secondary embargo to be GATT inconsistent. Again the United States refused to comply with the ruling. However, in 1995 the United States, along with Costa Rica, France, Mexico, Spain, and Venezuela, signed the Panama Declaration, an international agreement limiting the total number of dolphin deaths and also protecting sea turtles and certain small fish.[120] If this agreement is ratified by the U.S. Congress, American restrictions on tuna imports will be lifted.

As the tuna dispute was close to being resolved, two possible new U.S. trade sanctions to influence the marine conservation practices of its trading partners threatened to provoke additional trade disputes with the EU. The High Seas Drift Fisheries Enforcement Act of 1992 requires the United States to ban imports of fish and fish products from any nation that engages in large-scale driftnet fishing, a practice the United States considers highly destructive to marine life. The secretary of commerce has identified Italy as "a nation for which there is reason to believe that its nationals or vessels" are engaging in this fishing practice, and is considering imposing trade sanctions.[121]

Under another American marine conservation law that applies to both domestic and foreign fishing vessels, the United States has banned imports of shrimp from countries that cannot provide evidence that their shrimp fishermen have complied with American standards for turtle protection. Three EU member states—Italy, Spain, and Portugal—are among the countries potentially affected by this ban. Once again, the EU has protested vigorously against American unilateralism, which it said "may not necessarily be the appropriate means of achieving the objective of conservation and may be destablilizing for international trade."[122] The EU has emphasized the need for international cooperation to establish common standards. A WTO panel has been convened to hear this dispute.

Leg-Hold Traps

Despite its harsh criticism of American unilateralism, the EU has also moved to impose trade restrictions to influence the conservation practices of its trading partners, including the United States. In 1991 the European Council banned the use of leg-hold traps for catching wild animals within the EC. Beginning in 1995 it also prohibited imports of thirteen species of fur from nations that continue to use these traps rather than more humane trapping methods.[123]

This policy change stemmed from some of the same factors that had led to the hormone ban. First, the European Council was responding to an intense moral campaign by European animal rights activists similar to the one mounted by European consumer activists against beef and dairy cattle hormones. Second, Europeans regarded the import ban as critical to maintaining a single European market for furs because some member states wanted to prohibit the sale of furs harvested from leg-hold traps within their borders. Thus once again the EU's commitment to harmonize standards at a high level magnified the differences between U.S. and European standards. Third, the import ban was supported by domestic producers whose production techniques differed from their North American competitors. Europe's large pelt industry relies on animal farming rather than trapping. Moreover, in part because of antifur movements in a number of European countries, it had experienced a severe decline in sales.

The import ban was primarily aimed at the United States, Canada, and the former members of the Soviet Union, the main suppliers of wild animal pelts to the EU's fur industry. Approximately 70 percent of the furs harvested in North America are exported to Europe. The EU's decision provoked a particular outcry from Canada, where some 80,000 trappers earn more than $30 million a year from pelt exports to Europe.[124] Half these trappers are native Americans, many of whom depend on trapping for most of their income. A delegation of native Canadians accused the EU of committing "cultural genocide."[125]

Caught between pressures from the European Parliament and animal welfare groups on one hand and anxious to avoid a trade dispute with the United States and Canada on the other, in November 1995 the European Commission decided to postpone the import ban until January 1, 1997, to allow its trading partners to find a more humane alternative to leg-hold traps and reach agreement on an international standard for fur harvesting. The commission also exempted indigenous peoples from the ban.

This decision was immediately denounced by European animal welfare activists.[126] On December 14, 1995, the commission's action was condemned in the European Parliament by a vote of 262 to 46, and the Parliament called on the EU to institute a ban immediately. In language reminiscent of the response of American environmentalists to the GATT tuna decision, animal rights activists accused the commission of "sacrificing animals on the altar of free world trade."[127]

The European Commission has attempted to work closely with the International Standardization Organization to develop a definition of "inhumane traps," since according to the WTO Standards Code, a trade restriction based on an internationally recognized standard is more likely to pass WTO scrutiny. Indeed, the EU has publicly differentiated its ban on leg-hold traps from the American tuna embargo on precisely this basis. Although the ISO has yet to develop an international standard acceptable to the EU, leg-hold traps have been banned in eighty-eight countries. From this perspective the EU ban on the traps does reflect a greater international consensus than did the American requirement for dolphin protection.

Frustrated by the lack of progress on establishing an international standard, EU environment ministers again warned exporters that the EU would implement its ban in January 1997 unless discussions on finding an alternative to leg-hold traps produced satisfactory results.[128] They also announced their opposition to exempting indigenous peoples. One member state, the Netherlands, chose not to wait for the EU to act and instituted its own import ban on furs and skins from animals caught with leg-hold traps. The United States and Canada responded to the Dutch action by threatening to file a complaint with the WTO.[129]

In October 1996 EU negotiators proposed restricting their import ban to furs from animals caught in steel-jawed traps. The ban would be phased in over a period of three to five years. Padded leg-hold traps and aquatic traps would still be permitted, but their use would be closely monitored to determine if they caused high levels of damage or stress to animals. An EU diplomat said of the proposal, "A deal would represent a major movement towards accepting world-wide standards on human trapping."[130] Canada and Russia agreed to this compromise, but the United States did not. Neither was it acceptable to Great Britain's environment minister, who stated that the European Council was not prepared to distinguish among different kinds of traps. Once again the EU voted to delay the implementation of the import ban.[131] Thus the impasse continues.

Eco-Labeling

More recently, another European environmental initiative—eco-labeling—has become a source of transatlantic trade tension.

Like the leg-trap ban, this EU policy affects a number of other countries. National eco-labeling has emerged as an important instrument of environmental policy in Europe, where significant numbers of consumers are interested in purchasing environmentally friendly products. A 1995 survey reported that 82 percent of German consumers, 67 percent of Dutch consumers, and 50 percent of French and British consumers stated that they "incorporate environmental concerns in their shopping behavior."[132] According to another study, "67 percent of EU citizens had already purchased or were ready to buy 'green' products."[133] Eco-labeling offers European firms an important financial incentive to improve their environmental practices, and it enables them to do so while maintaining their market shares.

However, the EU has become concerned about the proliferation of national eco-labeling programs. Fifteen sets of member state labels, each using distinctive criteria and designating different products, could confuse consumers. Furthermore, if national labeling bodies employed criteria that favored domestic producers, eco-labeling could undermine the single European market. To address these problems, in 1992 the EU authorized a voluntary eco-label to be awarded to ecologically sensitive products that met objective environmental standards established at the EU level.[134]

This eco-label was intended not to replace the labels of the member states but to supplement them. However, the European Commission assumed that many manufacturers would prefer the eco-label because it would be recognized throughout the EU. Manufacturers were first required to apply to a national body in either the member state where the product was manufactured or where it was first imported. If their product met the appropriate environmental criteria, the manufacturers or distributors could use the eco-label throughout the EU. The European Commission was also instructed to provide for "cradle-to-grave" assessments: the ecological impact of each product would be evaluated throughout its production cycle, from the extraction of raw materials to its disposal after use.

The standards for awarding EU eco-labels are established jointly by the EU and the member states.[135] The EU decides which product categories are to be included in the program. It then assigns each to a member state, which conducts a life-cycle assessment based on a product's preproduction, production, distribution, use, and disposal. This lead country is responsible for developing product criteria based on its research. However, the product criteria must be approved by all member states to prevent any distortion of the single market. Member states are also responsible for processing applications for certification, awarding labels, and monitoring label use within their borders.

The establishment of Euro-labels has proceeded slowly, in part because of differences in consumer preferences, especially between the EU's northern, greener members and its poorer, less green southern members. EU eco-label criteria have been adopted and published for the following consumer product categories: refrigerators, washing machines, dishwashers, paper towels, toilet paper, laundry detergents, light bulbs, paints and varnishes, bed linens and T-shirts, photocopy paper, and soil improvers. However, only a handful of products with European eco-labels are actually on sale in Europe.[136] Some national representatives have suggested reducing the number of criteria for each product group in order to expedite the approval process.[137]

The EU's eco-labeling program has created tensions with a number of its trading partners, including the United States. In 1996 American officials held a number of meetings with their European counterparts to express concern about the lack of opportunities for meaningful participation by American firms in establishing the EU's eco-labeling criteria. They contended that the European system had a "potential for discrimination against U.S. firms whose production processes and methods differ from those used in the EU while having comparable environmental impacts." The Office of the U.S. Trade Representative listed the EU's eco-labeling scheme in its annual report to Congress under the "Super 301" program as "a topic of continuing concern."[138]

If a WTO complaint were to be filed by one of the EU's trading partners, it will most likely involve paper standards.[139] Wood pulp and paper producers from the United States, Canada, and Brazil have argued that the EU's criteria for "green" paper products constitute a nontariff trade barrier: they discriminate against foreign paper producers by placing primary emphasis on the use of recycled materials rather than on appropriate forest management. According to an official from the American Forest and Paper Association, "Just because a paper is recycled does not mean that it has less of an impact on the environment. We have programs on sustainable forestry that we feel are just as safe for the environment. . . . We feel that the Commission's criteria are in fact designed to subsidize the recycling industry in Europe."[140] The association claims that most U.S. suppliers will not qualify for a label without spending large sums of money. An article in *Newsweek* in the spring of 1996 highlighted the growing fears of American exporters about the EU's eco-labeling program:

> Paper recycling might make sense in Holland, but requiring paper made in Canada's sparsely settled west to use recycled pulp may consume more resources than it saves. Or take the EU's eco-label for T shirts. United States makers claim the rules permit more pollution from plants that dump wastewater into the sewer than do those that treat it on site, as most United States textile plants do.[141]

The EU's eco-labeling criteria have also come under strong criticism from third world countries, which fear that the labels will be employed as a form of "green protectionism." Thus, like the United States after its tuna import ban, the EU has found itself criticized by virtually all its trading partners.

Ironically, the EU's proposed standards have also been sharply attacked by European paper producers, who fear that what is now a voluntary scheme will shortly become a legal standard. The Confederation of European Paper Industries (CEPI) has questioned the environmental value of the EU's criteria for awarding eco-labels and claims that it discriminates against small, nonintegrated paper producers. While denying that it plans to boycott the labels, CEPI clearly hopes "no company will apply."[142]

The WTO's Trade and Environment Committee is examining the trade implications of the EU's eco-labeling plans and the WTO's consistency of eco-labeling standards. Specifically, it is attempting to reconcile the growth of eco-labels with the newly strengthened Standards Code, which commits all WTO signatories to ensure that "technical regulations and standards, par-

ticularly with respect to the packaging . . . and labeling of goods
. . . create no unnecessary obstacles to international trade."[143]

However, as in the case of the hormone ban before the Uruguay Round agreement, there is considerable debate about
whether the European eco-label falls within the scope of the
Standards Code.[144] The label is clearly not a "technical regulation" because compliance is voluntary. But because the EU is a
widely recognized organization and governments play an important, if informal, role in determining the criteria for awarding
eco-labels, its label could constitute a "standard," which would
bring it within the code's scope. This would mean that the EU
would be required to make its labels nondiscriminatory, transparent, and based whenever possible on international standards.
It would also be obligated to provide its trading partners with
the opportunity to comment on the criteria used to award the
labels. More important, because the label is based on a life-cycle
assessment, it might well violate the GATT's restrictions on the
use of environmental standards to influence the ways goods are
produced or processed outside a country's borders.

The United States is firmly convinced that the EU's eco-
labeling program "violates the law of international trade." According to U.S. Ambassador to the EU Stuart Eizenstat, the
American concern is "not with eco-labels per se. Our problem
is that the process is not sufficiently transparent and does not
allow for the participation of non-EU industries."[145] He added
that he was also worried about the problem of discrimination.
"We want to be able to show that if we have equivalent environmentally benign production processes, they should be given an
eco-label. Just because a United States process is different does
not mean that it is environmentally unsound. Our hope is that
this does not turn into a covert trade restriction by favoring EU
processes."

An American trade association official has described the EU's
eco-labeling program as "a very important issue not only for the
United States but for countries such as Canada and Brazil."[146]
An American trade lawyer characterized the EU's labeling standards as an "area of enormous potential conflict," adding that
"as we move toward international standardization of labeling,
Europe is going to be setting the agenda."[147] However, the United

States has not taken any formal legal action against the EU, largely because the European labeling programs have yet to adversely affect the sales of any American product in Europe.

The European Commission has proposed that the Standards Code be amended to permit the use of eco-labeling schemes based on a life-cycle approach, thus assuring the WTO of the consistency of its own scheme, an idea to which the United States is unlikely to agree. The ISO has begun work on international standards for eco-labels. These would emphasize "credibility, consultation with stakeholders, transparency, accessibility and avoiding the creation of unnecessary obstacles to trade."[148] Its work has been strongly supported by the United States and export-reliant developing countries that fear the use of eco-labels as trade barriers. But the development of international consensus on an ISO Standard on Environmental Labels and Declaration (Draft Standard 14020) has proved difficult. In particular, a number of national delegations, including those from the United Kingdom, Germany, and France, want the ISO's draft principles to serve as guidelines rather than standards, a position strongly opposed by the United States and Canada.[149]

There are, however, other ways of promoting international cooperation on eco-labeling. One is to employ the "principle of equivalency," which would permit a product to qualify for an eco-label if it met minimal or equivalent environmental standards, even if they were not identical to those of the country to which the product was exported. Another approach is "mutual recognition," which would mean that an importing country's eco-label could be awarded to any products covered by a national or regional eco-label. These approaches remain at the discussion stage.[150]

The stakes in this matter go beyond the use and methods of the EU's eco-labeling criteria. They touch one of the most important and contentious issues in the relationship between trade policy and environmental regulation: the extent to which it is appropriate for nations to regulate imported products on the basis of how they are produced or processed. This issue underlies the dispute not only over the EU's eco-labeling plan, but also the American tuna ban and the EU's leg-trap ban, both of which regulate the way imported products are produced. How this issue is addressed has serious consequences for the future of environmental regulation and trade. On the one hand, efforts to promote sustainable development require that nations be able to regulate how products are made or processed outside their borders. But on the other hand, restricting imports on the basis of production methods can threaten the basis of international trade, which rests in part precisely on national differences in the way goods are produced or harvested. It also can serve as a form of protectionism. Formulating new rules to address this critical issue is high on the agenda of the WTO's Trade and Environment Committee.

Chemical Testing

In contrast to the leg-trap ban and eco-labeling, in which the EU's efforts to maintain the single market have exacerbated trade tensions with the United States, in the case of chemical testing the creation of a single European market and regulatory cooperation between the EU and the United States have been mutually reenforcing. During the mid-1970s the European Community, responding to increased public concern about the environmental impact of chemicals, attempted to strengthen its standards for chemical safety. However agreement proved impossible because of differences between Europe's two main chemical producers, Great Britain and Germany. Neither was willing to surrender its national authority over the regulation of this important and politically powerful industry.

This deadlock was broken in 1976 by the passage of the Toxic Substances Control Act (TSCA) by the United States. This legislation, which established new requirements for the manufacture of all new and existing chemicals in the United States, created considerable anxiety on the part of European chemical producers: they feared it would undermine their ability to export their products to the United States. European officials recognized that their bargaining power would be significantly strengthened if they were able to reach agreement among themselves. In the spring of 1978 the European Commission asked the European Council for a formal mandate to negotiate with the United States and to develop parallel legislation. A year later, with the United States about to implement TSCA, the council approved the sixth amendment to the 1967 Framework Directive on Dangerous Substances. This established a European standard for the premarket notification of new chemicals based on a modified system of mutual recognition.

Following the approval of this amendment, the EU entered into negotiations with the United States under the auspices of the OECD. Although the OECD had been involved in coordinating chemical regulations since the early 1970s, the enactment of new, comprehensive, and divergent approaches to the screening of new chemical substances on both sides of the Atlantic lent considerable urgency to its efforts. European and American firms were responsible for the majority of international trade in chemicals. "Agreement on the basic contours of premarket notification packages would go far to ensure that the previously unfettered commerce in new industrial chemicals would not be impaired by conflicting or discriminatory regulatory controls."[151]

After extensive negotiations, in 1981 the OECD countries adopted the Decision of the Council Concerning the Mutual Acceptance of Data in the Assessment of Chemicals.[152] This agreement, which is binding on all OECD member countries, requires that the data generated in the testing of chemicals in any OECD member state be accepted in all other OECD countries for health, safety, and environmental assessment. To implement the agreement, the OECD's Environment Policy Committee has issued Test Guidelines, a common set of test methods for chemicals. The guidelines were developed by a network of national coordinators, one in each OECD country, who worked with teams of regulatory, academic, and industrial experts. Since 1981, eighty-four test guidelines have been adopted: they specify methodologies by which chemicals are to be tested for characteristics such as genetic toxicity, biodegradability, toxicity to fish, and so forth.

The adoption of these test guidelines remains optional, but any OECD country requiring that chemicals be tested for any of the characteristics addressed by the guidelines must accept the test results from other OECD countries, provided that the data were produced using the Test Guidelines methodologies. This means that any of the tests must only be conducted once. This agreement has not only facilitated trade in chemicals but has increased the generation of scientifically valid and high-quality test data and reduced the costs of chemical testing for both governments and the private sector. Equally important, it has established a mechanism for the creation of new international guidelines and the revision of existing ones.

The Montreal Protocol

The series of agreements that established and subsequently strengthened international standards to protect the ozone layer were negotiated primarily by the European Union and the United States. These agreements constitute one of the most important examples of U.S.-EU regulatory cooperation, one whose impact has extended far beyond the two entities.

The problem of ozone depletion first surfaced in the mid-1970s when a scientific paper theorized that the release of chlorofluorocarbons (CFCs) into the atmosphere could damage the ozone layer, which protects the earth from harmful ultraviolet rays. CFC production was concentrated in a relatively small number of countries, with the United States accounting for half of global production. In 1978 the United States responded to the increased public concern about ozone depletion by banning aerosol spray cans. During the 1980s, ozone protection emerged as the priority of the American environmental movement, which campaigned vigorously for additional regulations to curb domestic emissions of the chemical. In 1989 Congress enacted a substantial tax on the production of CFCs and halons, another ozone-depleting chemical primarily used in fire extinguishers.

Because only Canada, Norway, and Sweden followed the American lead in banning aerosol sprays, American firms found themselves at a competitive disadvantage. Moreover, as American exports of CFCs declined, CFC production in Europe increased. At the same time, domestic political pressures on the chemical industry continued to intensify. By the late 1980s, producers faced the possibility of a complete phaseout of CFC production. Anticipating much tighter restrictions, the American chemical firms, led by DuPont, which accounted for one-quarter of global CFC production, began investing substantial funds to develop a substitute for CFCs.

The American chemical industry now urged that any future regulatory actions by the United States be coordinated with those of other countries. Not only would a regulation banning CFC production in the United States alone be inadequate to protect the ozone layer, but such a unilateral action would "cause a US loss of world market share for goods and services . . . because products containing CFC substitutes [as proposed in domestic regulations] would not be acceptable in export markets because of their higher costs and incompatibility with foreign products."[153] The American government concurred and began to press actively for an international agreement.

During the late 1980s, German environmental groups began to urge their government to impose restrictions on domestic CFC production. Threatened with unilateral restrictions, the German chemical industry joined its American competitors in calling for an international phaseout. However, the EC remained divided about whether to support an international treaty. Belgium, Denmark, Germany, and the Netherlands favored such an agreement; Britain, France, and Italy were opposed. The British opposition to international controls reflected the interests of ICI, the nation's sole CFC producer, which exported one-third of its production. Once ICI began to make progress in developing CFC substitutes, the British position softened. What ultimately led the EC to join the Americans in supporting an international agreement was its fear that without a multilateral agreement, the United States would impose trade restrictions on imports of products containing CFCs.

Once the EC had a united position, negotiations with the United States began in earnest. The Montreal Protocol, which was adopted in 1987, called for a 50 percent reduction in CFCs by the end of the century. Two years later the timetable was accelerated: reflecting the growing political strength of green parties in much of Europe, the EC agreed to reduce CFC production by 85 percent as soon as possible. Following the 1993 Copenhagen amendments, the member states agreed to phase out all CFC production by 1995. The U.S. Environmental Protection Agency responded by advancing its phaseout timetable.

Although reductions in the production and use of other ozone-depleting chemicals such as methyl bromide will take place more slowly, progress in protecting the ozone layer has been made. One hundred forty-eight nations have ratified the Montreal Protocols and thirty-seven have accepted the Copenhagen amendments. Although compliance by a number of developing countries remains uneven, the Montreal Protocol and the various amendments do have an important enforcement mechanism: they provide for trade sanctions against exports from nations that have not agreed to sufficient reductions in their production of ozone-harming chemicals. They also provide for a fund, initially set at $160 million to $240 million, to assist developing countries in complying with their control obligations.

The Montreal Protocols demonstrate the critical need for international cooperation to address global environmental problems. No major chemical-producing nation could afford to impose substantial restrictions on domestic production without the assurance that those nations with whom its firms competed were prepared to do likewise. At the same time, restrictions at the national level were obviously inadequate to address what was clearly a global problem.

As in the case of the ICH and the OECD chemical testing guidelines, agreement on international regulatory standards was significantly facilitated by the fact that all large producers had similar interests, at least after they found themselves under comparable public pressure. All stood to benefit from international rather than regional or national standards. But the growth in the regulatory competency of the EC was also critical in making international agreement possible. Moreover, by magnifying the preferences of Germany, the EU's most important green member state, the EC's involvement resulted in international agreements to limit ozone depletion that were much stronger than what would likely have occurred had each member state negotiated with the United States on its own. Once again European economic integration strengthened regulatory standards, but in this case facilitating rather than reducing regulatory cooperation with the United States.

5

Conclusion

WHAT DO THE ILLUSTRATIONS of EU-U.S. regulatory relations presented here—the controversies over animal hormones, genetically engineered crops, meat inspection, pharmaceutical regulation and inspection, fuel economy standards, the tuna and leg-hold trap bans, eco-labeling, chemical testing standards, and ozone depletion—tell us about the dynamics of EU-U.S. regulatory cooperation and conflict?

Many critics of trade liberalization, which include a number of NGOs in both Europe and the United States, have expressed concern about the impact of increased international competition on regulatory standards. They have argued that this competition will cause a regulatory "race to the bottom" as nations lower their own standards to gain or maintain a competitive advantage. But the examples I have discussed provide no basis for these concerns. There does not appear to be a single instance in which either the United States or the EU lowered any health, safety, or environmental standard to make its domestic producers more competitive.[154]

On the contrary, standards have moved steadily, if unevenly, upward on both sides of the Atlantic. Indeed, it is precisely the strengthening of standards that has led to so many of the trade disputes I have described. The EU's beef and dairy hormone and leg-trap bans, as well as its eco-labeling standards, and the American CAFE regulations and its tuna import ban, all have been enacted during a period of intensified international competition. The same dynamic holds true within the EU itself. Its progress in creating a single market, especially since the passage of the Single European Act (1987), has been accompanied by

increasingly stringent health, safety, and environmental standards for a number of traded goods, including meat, furs, and
chemicals.

To what extent have trade tensions between the United States
and the EU stemmed from the enactment of more stringent regulations designed to create a competitive advantage? Have they
used health, safety, and environmental regulations as a means
of protecting their markets from each other? It is certainly true
that a number of new, more stringent U.S. and EU social regulations have left importers at a disadvantage—if the regulations
had not done so, they would not have become the focus of trade
disputes. But while they benefited domestic producers, which
may well have facilitated their adoption, that was not the primary reason most were enacted. There is little evidence that
firms in either the United States or the EU have intentionally
sought to use health, safety, or environmental regulations as
nontariff barriers.

It was not European cattle ranchers who urged the EU to ban
the use of hormones to keep out American products. In fact
many cattle farmers in the EU strongly opposed such a ban.
Neither European food retailers nor food processers stand to
gain a competitive advantage by insisting on labeling food produced from genetically engineered crops. Obviously, some European farmers will benefit from regulations that limit sales of
bioengineered crops, as will the European fur industry from the
ban on imports of furs harvested with leg-hold traps. But neither
regulatory proposal or policy was initiated by European producers. Moreover, many European firms have been as critical of the
EU's eco-labeling programs as have foreign producers. For their
part, CAFE standards have always been strongly opposed by the
American automobile industry on the grounds that they are
costly and force the manufacturers to produce large numbers of
smaller, lighter cars that Americans are uninterested in purchasing. The tuna import ban was neither initiated nor supported by the American tuna industry, which had no need of
import protection because its dolphin-safe tuna commanded a
considerable premium on the American market. The BST ban
represents a partial exception to this generalization because it

was primarily enacted by the EU to protect European dairy farmers. But the ban has also been strongly supported by European consumer groups.

Why were these regulations proposed or adopted? In virtually every case, the key reason was pressures from NGOs or public opinion. Thus the EU's ban on leg-hold traps and the American tuna embargo were initiated by animal rights activists and environmentalists respectively. Likewise, the EU's beef and dairy hormone bans and its labeling of genetically engineered foods were a response to pressures from European consumers. The eco-labeling initiatives reflect the intensity of public support in much of Europe for improving environmental quality. The CAFE standard was approved by Congress as a response to the widespread public anxiety about energy conservation in the aftermath of the 1973 Mideast oil embargo. Indeed, it is precisely because the enactment of these regulations was not primarily driven by the interests of producers seeking protection that resolving the trade disputes created by them has proved so difficult.

The political institutions of both the EU and the United States have magnified these public pressures. Commitment to the single market led the EU to harmonize regulations for hormones, animal furs, and eco-labeling. Having been driven to establish a common standard to avoid undermining the single market for goods that were widely traded in Europe, it had to decide which standard to enact. Given the political strength of environmental and consumer groups in the EU's most powerful member states, it was more politically expedient to require that others raise their standards than it was to force the EU's greener member states to lower them. And once having imposed the standards on domestic producers, it sought to impose them on foreign ones as well.

Thus the creation of the single market has exacerbated trade tensions with the United States by increasing the leverage of Europe's greener nations over a wide range of European regulatory policies, many of which affect American producers. For example, had the decisions on hormone use been left to each member state, American beef producers would have been able to export their products to some European nations. The same holds true for American exports of furs, since some countries in Europe are indifferent to the issue of animal protection. The citizens of the various member states are not equally anxious about the consumption of bioengineered food. Likewise, were the enactment of eco-labeling standards left to each member state, some would choose not to develop them.

In the United States the access of NGOs to the regulatory process has also contributed to EU-U.S. regulatory trade tensions. A lawsuit filed by an American environmental organization resulted in both the primary and secondary tuna embargoes. The strongest supporters of CAFE standards, domestically and internationally, have been America's politically influential consumer and environmental organizations. Likewise, environmental groups have been the most prominent backers of trade sanctions to protect marine life outside America's borders.

The persistence of regulations as sources of trade tension between the United States and the EU reflects an important similarity between them. Both are relatively affluent democratic societies in which many citizens place a high value on environmental and consumer protection. But their common values also divide them. Both find themselves under constant pressure to impose additional regulations on industry to advance a wide and ever changing variety of public goals. Both remain on the cutting edge of environmental and consumer regulation. Technology and public pressures have led to a continually expanding regulatory agenda: labeling bioengineered products, eco-labeling, the use of leg-hold traps, the protection of turtles—all are issues that did not exist even a few years ago.

However, for a variety of cultural and political reasons, citizens and NGOs on both sides of the Atlantic do not share identical goals or priorities. Although some American consumer groups are no less critical than their European counterparts of the health impacts of various agricultural technologies, they have not challenged the use of hormones in beef production or demanded the labeling of genetically engineered food. American consumers who prefer hormone-free beef do so by consuming beef products that have been so labeled; they have not campaigned to change all American beef production. Likewise,

American animal rights activists are by no means less vocal than their counterparts across the Atlantic, but they have focused their political energies on banning or restricting the use of animals in laboratory tests rather than outlawing the use of traps to catch wild animals. They have also placed a greater priority on protecting dolphins and turtles than other wild animals.

Another source of trade tensions between the United States and the European Union stems not from differences in policy objectives but from the methods used to achieve them. For example, the United States does not place a higher value on fuel conservation than the EU does. Indeed, because the American fuel economy standards result in less energy savings than the much higher taxes on gasoline that are common throughout Europe, the U.S. commitment to energy conservation is actually much weaker. But because of domestic political opposition to increased taxes, the United States has chosen to promote energy conservation through CAFE standards.

The same holds true of the American ban on tuna imports to protect dolphins. The EU's objection is to the American reliance on unilateral sanctions rather than international agreements to achieve this objective. Likewise, the EU eco-labeling program does not reflect a greater interest in "green" consumption on the part of European consumers. Although no quasi-official standards for eco-labeling have been developed at either the national or state level in the United States, green marketing is just as extensive in the United States as it is in much of Europe.

Still, it is important to recognize that underlying a number of U.S.-EU trade disputes are deeply held and widely divergent social and cultural values. To take one of the most important examples, food "purity" is more important to Europeans than it is to Americans: thus the EU's ban on beef hormones and BST and support for labeling bioengineered agricultural products. Indeed, transatlantic differences in food safety regulations both reflect and have contributed to fundamental differences in agricultural policy. Americans have sought to sustain agriculture by introducing new productivity-enhancing technologies; Europeans have chosen precisely the opposite strategy: they have sought to protect farmers by restricting the use of new agricultural technologies. Any effort to harmonize regulations in these visible and emotional areas is likely to prove highly divisive, if not fruitless. Trade disputes resulting from such differences are unlikely ever to be resolved; at best they can be contained.

Industry and government officials on both sides of the Atlantic need to approach the challenge of regulatory cooperation carefully and selectively. Once differences in particular regulatory policies or procedures become highly politicized, resolving them becomes much more difficult. An important reason for the progress made by the ICH and the OECD in promoting cooperation in testing standards for new drugs and chemicals is that their deliberations have taken place outside the public spotlight. No political controversy has accompanied the approval or banning of a particular drug or chemical on one side of the Atlantic or the other. There is no pharmaceutical or chemical equivalent to beef hormones or BST. There has been relatively little public interest in the negotiations aimed at promoting mutual recognition of veterinary and pharmaceutical inspection standards, and these negotiations have, at last, achieved substantial results. More generally, mutual acceptance of testing and inspection requirements is likely to prove more politically feasible than harmonizing regulatory standards, at least for products that raise highly visible health, safety, or environmental concerns.

The intensity of so many U.S.-EU trade disputes is striking. In contrast to many other regions or countries neither has made deliberate use of regulations as trade barriers.[155] And in marked contrast to Japan, the regulations enacted by the United States and the EU have been transparent, thus considerably facilitating efforts to reduce their function as trade barriers. The conflicts described in this study by no means exhaust the list of EU and U.S. health, safety, and environmental regulations that have been alleged to interfere with market access. But even if virtually every regulation and requirement that has been cited by either side as an obstacle or barrier to trade were removed, the increase in trade flows across the Atlantic would be modest.

Transatlantic trade totals $250 billion, the second largest bilateral trade flow in the world. (Only U.S.-Canada trade is larger, by a narrow margin.)[156] It is also generally balanced: in some years the EU has a modest surplus, in others the United States. Most important, it is steadily growing. Thus by any measure, the United States and the EU are increasingly open to each other's products and services. Why then have their regulation-related trade disputes been so contentious?

The answer is that their respective regulatory policies loom so significant because each is such an important market to the other. Each new regulation or rule that appears to disadvantage importers, no matter how economically unimportant, becomes magnified in its potential scope. Indeed, it is precisely because the playing field is relatively level that each rule or regulation that disadvantages importers becomes of immediate concern to producers on both sides of the Atlantic. Each fears that unless it is immediately and effectively challenged it will establish a dangerous precedent that will be used to justify other trade restrictions, further limiting access to an extremely important market. Equally important, because both U.S. and EU regulatory policies are often adopted by other countries, producers worry that new rules will spread, compounding their economic impact.

The same logic holds true for NGOs on both sides of the Atlantic. They, too, regard each challenge to a regulation they support as a precedent that will then be used to challenge numerous other regulations, not only in the United States or the EU but in other countries. In short, both producers and NGOs regard the use of regulations that restrict trade, as well as the challenges to them, as a slippery slope. This helps explain, for example, the intensity of American fur trappers' opposition to the ban on leg-hold traps and the support for this ban by European animal rights activists. A similar dynamic holds true for the American CAFE standard. It was characterized as a dangerous precedent by the EU, while the challenge to it provoked an equally heated response by American environmental groups. The same conflicting interests and values underlie support for and opposition to the American ban on tuna imports and the EU's ban on beef and dairy hormones.

The United States and the EU should not be overly preoccupied with minimizing trade friction by harmonizing every regulatory standard, policy, and procedure. International regulatory diversity has an important value: it can help promote the gradual tightening of regulations as each trading partner raises its standards in response to actions of the other. For example, the gradual raising of European automotive emission standards can be seen in part as a response to actions by the United States. Moreover, regulatory harmonization can be counterproductive if it is based on faulty methodology or data: there would be little point in having either the United States or the EU adopt each other's least scientifically defensible regulatory standards in order to facilitate trade between them.

The United States and the EU face two primary trading challenges. The first is to continue to make steady progress in reducing the role of consumer and environmental standards as obstacles to trade while respecting legitimate substantive differences in regulatory policies. Such reductions have taken a variety of forms short of harmonization, including mutual acceptance of equivalent standards, mutual recognition of testing standards, mutual recognition of conformity assessment and the exchange of technical information by regulatory authorities. Each requires trust among regulatory officials, which has taken time to develop. The various highly publicized trade disputes between the EU and the United States described in this study should not allow us to overlook their steady progress in regulatory cooperation.

The second challenge is for the United States and the EU to place their relationship in perspective. Both need to understand their agreements and disagreements in an international context. What is striking about the three most important cases of EU-U.S. cooperation explored here—the agreements reached by the OECD, ICH, and Montreal Protocol—is that they took place within a multilateral framework. The progress the United States and the EU made on regulatory cooperation occurred as part of a much broader effort to harmonize global regulatory standards and procedures. At the same time, multilateral agreements have helped reduce EU-U.S. trade tensions. Thus the newly strengthened Standards Code promises to resolve the fifteen-year dispute over the EC's ban on beef hormones, while the interests of both sides in avoiding a WTO dispute settlement panel may well contribute to an international standard that will resolve the trade dispute over the EU's ban on leg-hold traps. In this sense the growing use of the WTO dispute mechanisms by the EU and the United States represents an extremely important development.

WTO panels may come to adjudicate trade disputes over health, safety, and environmental regulations analogous to the critical role played by the European Court of Justice within the European Union.

Whether progress toward international regulatory cooperation is motivated by the goal of reducing obstacles to trade or strengthening the effectiveness of regulatory standards, the most important challenge for the United States and the EU is to promote regulatory cooperation at the global level. This cooperation is critical not only to reduce the use of health, safety, and environmental regulations as disguised forms of protectionism, but to promote the global diffusion of more effective government regulation. The real challenge is to develop an international regulatory regime that incorporates Japan as well as the developing nations. That is where the greatest obstacles as well as the most important opportunities for international regulatory cooperation lie.

The United States and the EU are in a pivotal position to play a more active leadership role in defining and constructing such a regime. Their bilateral relationship can be considered a vehicle for developing new approaches to the achievement of international regulatory cooperation. In fact, standards on which the United States and the EU agree are increasingly likely to become accepted by other nations, thus becoming de facto international standards. This is clearly illustrated by the pattern of global trade liberalization since World War II; each successive GATT round promoting trade liberalization was made possible by an agreement between the United States and the EU, including the Uruguay Round agreement to limit the use of technical regulations as trade barriers. The same holds true for the adoption of global environmental treaties. This means, for example, that a consensus between the United States and the EU will be critical to an effective international agreement on global climate change or to change WTO rules to clarify the role of eco-labeling. Only after the EU and the United States have reached a common understanding do such global agreements become possible. Alternatively, in the absence of cooperation between the two, the prospects for international accord are dim.

Rather than focus so much energy on increasing their access

to each other's markets, the United States and the EU need to place more emphasis on identifying their common interests in fostering global regulatory cooperation. They need to pay more attention to their mutual interests in promoting international trade and improving the efficiency and effectiveness of regulatory standards around the world than to their differences over regulatory policies, priorities, and procedures. This does not make the bilateral relationship between them any less important. On the contrary, it makes it more so.

Notes

1. C. Fred Bergsten, "The Dollar and the Euro," *Foreign Affairs* (July–August 1997), p. 93.

2. Suzanne Berger, "Introduction," in Suzanne Berger and Ronald Dore, eds., *National Diversity and Global Capitalism* (Cornell University Press, 1996), p. 16.

3. Quoted in David Vogel, *Trading Up: Consumer and Environmental Regulation in A Global Economy* (Harvard University Press, 1995), p. 136.

4. Alan Sykes, *Product Standards for Internationally Traded Goods Markets* (Washington: Brookings, 1995), p. 124.

5. Ibid., p. 126.

6. *Regulatory Co-operation for an Interdependent World* (Paris: OECD, 1994), p. 142.

7. Quoted in George Bermann, "Regulatory Cooperation between the European Commission and U.S. Administrative Agencies," *Administrative Law Journal*, vol. 9 (1996), p. 935.

8. Horst Siebert, "TAFTA: Fueling Trade Discrimination or Global Liberalization?" American Institute for Contemporary German Studies seminar paper 19, March 1996, p. 4.

9. *Report on United States Barriers to Trade and Investment* (Brussels: Services of the European Commission, 1995), pp. 2–4.

10. Bermann, "Regulatory Cooperation," p. 972.

11. Quoted in ibid., p. 956.

12. For the most recent reports, see *Report on United States Barriers to Trade and Investment*; and *1992: Implementing the European Community Single Market: Sixth Followup Report* (USITC, January 1994).

13. Bermann, "Regulatory Cooperation," pp. 957–58.

14. "Transatlantic Regulatory Cooperation," paper from the European Commission to the EU-U.S. Sub-Cabinet meeting on May 22–23, 1996, p. 1.

15. Ibid., p. 1.

16. Office of the United States Trade Representative, *1996 National Trade Estimate, European Union* (1997).

17. Transatlantic Business Dialogue, "TABD Priorities for Mid-Year U.S.-EU Summit," May 13, 1997, p. 5.

18. Transatlantic Business Dialogue, "Chicago Declaration," November 9, 1996, p. 2.

19. Transatlantic Business Dialogue, "TABD Priorities," p. 3.

20. Brian Coleman, "U.S., EU Draft Pact on Trade-Product Standards," *Wall Street Journal*, May 29, 1997, p. A2.

21. Quoted in Bermann, "Regulatory Cooperation," p. 977.

22. Andre Brand and Amanda Ellerton, *Report on Hormone-Treated Meat* (Club de Bruxelles, 1989), p. 2.9.

23. Ibid, p. 3.4.

24. Quoted in Adrien Rafael Halpern, "The U.S.-EC Hormone Beef Controversy and the Standards Code: Implications for the Application of Health Regulations to Agricultural Trade," *North Carolina Journal of International Law and Commercial Relations*, vol. 14 (Winter 1989), p. 137.

25. Marl Hunter, "Francois Lamy: How France's Nader Won Ban on Hormone-Treated Meat," *Washington Post*, December 25, 1988, p. H3.

26. Quoted in Walter Mossberg, "Dispute over Meat Imports Threatens New Snarl in U.S.-E.C. Trade Links," *Wall Street Journal*, December 23, 1988, p. A4.

27. Quoted in "European Officials Emphasize Hormone Ban Is a Consumer Protection Issue, Not a Trade Barrier," *International Trade Reporter*, February 15, 1989, p. 197.

28. Ibid., p. 196.

29. Brand and Ellerton, *Report on Hormone-Treated Meat*, p. 3.3.

30. "Brie and Hormones," *Economist*, January 7, 1989, p. 21.

31. Ibid.

32. Brand and Ellerton, *Report on Hormone-Treated Meat*, p. 3.6.

33. "Environmental Protection Agency Pursuing 'More Aggressive' Role in Pesticide Trade," *International Trade Reporter*, vol. 7 (April 1990), p. 468.

34. Ibid.

35. "Executive Summary," Twentieth Session of the Joint FAO/WHO Codex Alimentarius Commission, July 13, 1993, p. 3.

36. James Harding, "UN food ruling sparks EU ire," *Financial Times*, July 14, 1995, p. 2.

37. Steve Charnovitz, "The World Trade Organization and Environmental Supervision," *International Trade Reporter*, June 26, 1994, p. 90.

38. Caroline Southey, "EU to rethink meat hormone ban," *Financial Times*, November 22, 1995, p. 4.

39. "EU defends ban on beef treated with hormones," *Financial Times*, January 14, 1996, p. 3.

40. Guy de Jonquires, "US files WTO case over EU beef ban," *Financial Times*, January 27–28, 1996, p. 3.

41. Caroline Southey, "EU reaffirms ban on meat hormones over US objection, *"Financial Times*, March 19, 1996, p. 6.

42. Bruce Clark, "US hails EU beef imports ruling by WTO," *Financial Times*, May 10, 1997, p. 2.

43. Edmund Andrews, "Europe's Banning of Treated Beef Is Ruled Illegal," *New York Times*, May 2, 1997, p. A1.

44. Clark, "US hails EU beef imports ruling by WTO," p. 2; and "France to keep US meat ban," *Financial Times*, May 12, 1997, p. 3.

45. Neil Buckley, "Brussels to appeal over hormones," *Financial Times*, July 2, 1997, p. 6.

46. Bruce Barnard, "Cease-Fire Ends in Hormone War between US, EC," *Journal of Commerce*, February 7, 1990, p. 5A.

47. "Note," *Food Chemical News*, December 12, 1988, p. 10.

48. Janet Shaner, "Beef Hormone Dispute," Harvard Business School Case no. 9-590-035, Rev. 12/89, p. 9.

49. Nancy Dunne, "Phony Peace Breaks Out in US-EC Clash over Farm Trade," *Financial Times*, April 27, 1989, p. D6.

50. Keith Rockwell, "US Says EC Milk Ban Would Set Bad Precedent," *Journal of Commerce*, August 7, 1989, p. 6A.

51. Ibid.

52. Ibid.

53. Quoted in "Trading Our Future?" Press Release, League of Rural Voters, undated, p. 4.

54. United States International Trade Commission, *1992, The Effect of Great Economic Integration within the European Community on the United States*, first follow-up report (March 1992), p. 6-49.

55. "US loses milk hormone vote," *Financial Times*, June 26, 1997, p. 7.

56. See, for example, Margaret Studer, "Genetic Engineering Is Resisted in Europe," *Wall Street Journal*, October 3, 1994, p. A15B; and Bruce Dorminey, "Suicidal spuds," *Financial Times*, April 22, 1997, p. 13.

57. Jorl Bleifuss, "Recipe for Disaster," *In These Times*, November 11, 1996, p. 13.

58. "Europe ambivalent on biotechnology," *Nature*, vol. 387 (June 26, 1997), p. 8.

59. Julie Wolf, "Europe Turns Up Nose at Biotech Food," *Wall Street Journal*, January 2, 1997, p. 8.

60. Alison Maitland, "Call for ban on biotech beans," *Financial Times*, October 8, 1996, p. 2.

61. Joe Rogaly, "Beans and genes," *Financial Times*, December 7–8, 1997, sec. 2, p. 1.

62. Scott Kilman, "European Food Retailers Want Notice of Genetically Engineered Crops," *New York Times*, May 30, 1997, p. A2.

63. Ibid., p. A12.

64. Neil Buckley, "EU food labeling rules approved," *Financial Times*,

January 17, 1997, p. 2; and Buckley, "Brussels defends maize ruling," *Financial Times*, April 10, 1997, p. 3.

65. Maggie Urry, "Genetic products row worsens," *Financial Times*, June 20, 1997, p. 4.

66. "The green gene giant," *Economist*, April 26, 1997, p. 66.

67. "Labelling the mutant tomato," *Economist*, August 9, 1997, p. 54. See also Neil Buckley, "EU to order genetic food labelling," *Financial Times*, August 4, 1997, p. 14.

68. Quoted in United States International Trade Commission, *1992, The Effect of Great Economic Integration*, p. 6-51.

69. United States International Trade Commission, *1991, The Effect of Great Economic Integration within the European Community on the United States*, third follow-up report (March 1991), p. 4-20.

70. United States International Trade Commission, *1992, The Effect of Great Economic Integration within the European Community on the United States*, fourth follow-up report (April 1992), p. 5-36.

71. Nancy Dunne, "US set to block EU exports of meat after talks fail," *Financial Times*, April 2, 1997, p. 1.

72. Nancy Dunne, "EU's deal with US averts food trade war," *Financial Times*, May 2, 1997, p. 6.

73. For a more detailed discussion of developments in the harmonization of pharmaceutical regulation, both within the EU and internationally, see David Vogel "The Globalization of Pharmaceutical Regulation," *Governance* (forthcoming).

74. Daniel Green, "Fast track to approval," *Financial Times*, April 24, 1997, p. vi.

75. Rosemary Kanusky, "Pharmaceutical Harmonization in the United States, the European Economic Community and Japan," *Houston Journal of International Law*, vol. 16 (1994), p. 689.

76. David Jordan, "International Regulatory Harmonization: A New Era in Prescription Drug Approval," *Vanderbilt Journal of Transnational Law*, vol. 25 (1992), pp. 490, 495.

77. See David Vogel, "When Consumers Oppose Consumer Protection: The Politics of Regulatory Backlash," *Journal of Public Policy* (October–December 1990), pp. 458–61. For data on the drug lag, see *Proposals to Reform Drug Regulation Law* (Washington: American Enterprise Institute, 1979).

78. Julie C. Relihan, "Expediting FDA Approval," *Boston University International Law Journal*, vol. 13 (1996), p. 251.

79. Jordan, "International Regulatory Harmonization," p. 492.

80. Relihan, "Expediting FDA Approval," p. 256. See also Jordan, "International Regulatory Harmonization," p. 496.

81. Jordan, "Prescription Drug Approval," p. 492.

82. Ibid., p. 493.

83. The previous standard, "lethal dose 50," would increase doses administered to laboratory animals until 50 percent of the animals died. Iron-

ically, this testing phase lasted longest for drugs that had the safest toxicity levels.

84. "A faster track for new drugs," *Financial Times*, December 9, 1991, p. 20.

85. "EC, USA and Japan Ready to Reduce Pharmaceutical Product-testing and Animal Tests Drastically," *Rapid*, Commission of the European Communities, November 13, 1991.

86. Jordan, "International Regulatory Harmonization," p. 495.

87. Quoted in Joseph Contrera, "Comment: The Food and Drug Administration and the International Conference on Harmonization: How Harmonious Will International Pharmaceutical Regulations Become?" *Administrative Law Journal*, vol. 9 (Winter 1995), p. 929.

88. Dan Kidd, "The International Conference on Pharmaceutical Regulations, the European Medicines Evaluation Agency, and the FDA: Who's Zooming Who?" *Indiana Journal of Global Legal Studies*, vol. 4 (Fall 1997), p. 5.

89. "ICH—A Great Success," *Daily News Biotechnology and Medical Technology,* December 11, 1995, p. 1.

90. Bermann, "Regulatory Cooperation," p. 964.

91. "Impact of First ICH Guidelines," *Information Access Company Newsletter Database*, October 30, 1995, p. 1.

92. "Euro Commission, EMEA Consider Global Dossier," *IAC Industry Express*, June 6, 1996, p. 1.

93. "Better Medicine to be Side-Effect of New Network," *Nikkei Weekly*, May 6, 1996, p. 1.

94. Jill Wechsler, "Washington vs. the World?" *Pharmaceutical Executive* (February 1966), p. 16.

95. "EEC/US/Japan: Major Agreement on Pharmaceutical Trials," *European Environment*, vol 3 (November 26, 1991), p. 1.

96. Linda Horton, "The Food and Drug Administration's International Harmonization, Enforcement, and Trade Policy Activities," *Fundamentals of Law and Regulation* (1997), p. 106.

97. "FDA Challenged by its Involvement in International Harmonization Efforts," *BNA Health Care Daily,* January 19, 1996, p. 1.

98. Morton Mintz, "Remembering Thalidomide," *Washington Post National Weekly Edition*, July 22, 1996, p. 21.

99. Eric M. Katz, "Europe's Centralized New Drug Procedures: Is the United States Prepared to Keep Pace?" *Food and Drug Law Journal*, vol. 48 (July 1993), pp. 585–86.

100. Jill Wechsler, "Tangled threads snarl harmonization," *Pharmaceutical Executive*, September 15, 1995, p. 18.

101. Contrera, "Comment," p. 947.

102. Wechsler, "Washington vs. the World?" p. 20.

103. Marianne Lavelle, "Free Trade vs. Law," *National Law Journal*, March 29, 1993, p. 39.

104. Ibid.

105. John Griffiths, "Fuel economy rule may hit Jaguar," *Financial Times*, February 28, 1983, p. 1.

106. Vogel, *Trading Up*, p. 132.

107. "US Auto Fuel-Efficiency Taxes to be Examined by GATT Panel," *News and Views from the GATT*, June 3, 1993, p. 4.

108. "U.S. Blocks EC Bid for GATT Dispute Panel on Car Tax," *Reuters European Business Report*, March 24, 1993, p. 1.

109. See for example, Doron P. Levin, "Detroit's Assault on Mileage Bill," *New York Times*, May 11, 1991, p. D1.

110. Dunne, "EC challenge," p. 5.

111. Peter Behr, "Trade Case Could Endanger Environmental Law, GATT," *Washington Post*, June 10, 1994, p. F1.

112. "GATT Rules against CAFE, Opens Door to Conservation Exception," *Inside US Trade*, October 4, 1994, p. S-1.

113. Ibid., p. S-7.

114. U.S. International Trade Commission, *Report on US Barriers, 1995*, p. 40.

115. John Maggs, "EC Will Protest United States Tuna Embargo against 20 Nations," *Journal of Commerce*, February 4, 1992, p. 3A.

116. Quoted in Robert Housman and Durwood Zaelke, "The Collision of the Environment and Trade: The GATT Tuna/Dolphin Decision," *Environment Law Reporter* (April 1992), p. 10274.

117. "Action Urged on Tuna Panel Report," *GATT Focus*, no. 88 (March 1992), p. 5.

118. Ibid.

119. Jonathan Marshall, "How Ecology Is Tied to Mexico Trade Pact," *San Francisco Chronicle*, February 25, 1992, p. A8.

120. "Tuna Fishing," European News Service, November 24, 1995.

121. U.S. International Trade Commission, *Report on U.S. Barriers, 1996*, p. 36.

122. U.S. International Trade Commission, *Report on U.S. Barriers, 1995*, p. 36.

123. Barnard Simon, "Hunting for a kinder kill," *Financial Times*, December 13, 1991, p. 2.

124. Ibid.

125. Caroline Southey, "Brussels gives way in fur trapping row," *Financial Times*, November 23, 1995, p. 4.

126. "EU/Canada/US/Russia: Commission Caught in Leg-hold Trap," *European Environment*, January 8, 1996.

127. "Commission Faces Court Action concerning Fur Imports," *Agency Europe*, January 16, 1996.

128. "EU warns of fur trap ban," *Financial Times*, March 3, 1996, p. 5.

129. "EU sets deadline on leg-hold traps," U.P.I., March 4, 1996.

130. Caroline Southey, "EU close to ending row over 'inhumane' traps," *Financial Times*, November 29, 1996, p. 4.

131. Caroline Southey, "EU and US head for fur trade showdown," *Financial Times*, December 10, 1996, p. 6.

132. Barry Rosen and George Sloane III, "Environmental Product Standards, Trade and European Consumer Goods Marketing," *Columbia Journal of World Business*, vol. 30 (Spring 1995), p. 76.

133. Public Relations Newswire, February 18, 1996, p. 1.

134. Paul Bristow, "The European Community Eco-Labelling Scheme," in *Life-Cycle Management and Trade* (Paris: OECD 1994), pp. 50–55.

135. "Profile of the EU Eco-Label Program," in *Guarding the Green Choice: A National Wildlife Federation Trade and Environment Report* (Washington: National Wildlife Federation, 1966), pp. 13–14.

136. James Harding, "Sticking point for fresh green products," *Financial Times*, March 29, 1995, p. 10.

137. "EU Launches Review of Ecolabel Scheme," *Environment Watch, Western Europe*, vol. 5 (February 16, 1996), pp. 11–12.

138. Venna Jha and Simonetta Zarrilli, "Eco-Labeling Initiatives as Potential Barriers to Trade," in *Life-Cycle Management*, pp. 64–73.

139. Ibid.

140. See "EU to Push Ahead with Eco-Labels for Paper Despite United States Objections," *BNA International Reporter*, vol. 13 (June 5, 1996), p. 935.

141. Marc Levinson, "Seeing Red over Green: Why Big Business Hates Eco-Labels," *Newsweek*, June 17, 1996, p. 55.

142. Caroline Southey and Bernard Simon, "Eco-labelling plans upset paper makers," *Financial Times*, August 26, 1996, p. 2.

143. Ibid.

144. Ibid.

145. Joe Kirwin, "Eizenstat Sees Room for Improvement in United States' Relations with EU," *BNA International Trade Reporter*, March 13, 1996, p. 447.

146. "Business Leaders Draft Proposals for U.S.-EU Trans-Atlantic Summit," *BNA International Trade Reporter*, May 29, 1996, p. 884. Available on Nexus.

147. "Attorney Says Environmental Trends Abroad Will Have Far-Reaching Impact on United States Firms," *BNA International Environment Daily*, October 19, 1995, p. 1.

148. Statement of Belinda Collins, director of the Office of Standards Services, National Institute of Standards and Technology, Department of Commerce before the House Science Committee Subcommittee on Technology, June 4, 1996. Federal Information Systems Corporation, Federal News Service. Available on Nexus.

149. "EU Members Unhappy at Draft Ecolabel Standard," *Environment Watch, Western Europe*, vol. 5 (April 5, 1996), pp. 1–2.

150. "UN Agencies Plan Labeling Scheme for Third World Products," *Environment Watch, Western Europe,* vol. 4 (March 4, 1994), p. 1.

151. Ronald Brickman, Sheila Jasanoff, and Thomas Ilgen, *Controlling Chemicals: The Politics of Regulation in Europe and the United States* (Cornell University Press, 1985), p. 282.

152. OECD Secretariat, "Lessons for Regulatory Co-operation: The Case of the OECD Test Guidelines Programme," in *Regulatory Co-Operation for an Interdependent World* (Paris: OECD, 1994), p. 142.

153. Written statement of E. Blanchard, a Dupont executive, in *Ozone Layer Depletion,* Hearing before the Subcommittee on Health and the Environment of the House Committee on Energy and Commerce, 100 Cong. 1 sess. (Government Printing Office, March 9, 1987), p. 300.

154. For a more extended discussion of the role of trade liberalization in raising regulatory standards, which I have labeled the "California effect" in part due to the role of California emission standards in strengthening automotive standards in Germany and throughout the EC, see Vogel, *Trading Up.*

155. See, for example, David Vogel, "Consumer Protection and Protectionism in Japan," *Journal of Japanese Studies,* vol. 18, no. 1 (1992), pp. 119–54.

156. Coleman, "U.S., EU Draft Pact on Trade-Product Standards," p. A2.

Index

Administrative Procedures Act
(U.S.), 10
Agreement on Sanitary and
Phytosanitary Measures (SPS),
20–21
Agreement on Technical Barriers to
Trade (Standards Code): beef
hormone trade dispute, 19, 64;
described, 5–6, 7; Dunkel draft,
20; eco-labeling trade dispute,
49–51; leg-hold trap trade
dispute, 46. *See also* General
Agreement on Tariffs and Trade
Agricultural biotechnology:
Europe-U.S. cultural differences,
22, 26, 60–62; U.S. competitive
advantages, 24. *See also* Beef
trade dispute; Bioengineered
crops trade dispute; Bovine
somatotropin (BST) trade dispute
American Cyanamid, 25
American Forest and Paper
Association, 49
American Meat Industry Trade
Policy Council, 29
American National Cattlemen's
Beef Association, 22
Andriessen, Frans, 16–17
Animal products trade disputes, 2;
beef hormones, 15–24, 58, 64;
bovine somatotropin (BST), 24–
26, 58–59, 63; meat inspection
standards, 28–31

Argentina, 17
Australia, 20, 21–22
Austria, 28

Bangemann, Martin, 9
Beef trade dispute, 58, 64; Council
of Ministers hormone ban, 15–
17; U.S. beef exports to Europe,
17, 19, 23; U.S. objections to
hormone ban, 2, 17–19, 21, 23–
24; World Trade Organization
ruling, 3, 21–23
Belgium, 55
Bioengineered crops trade dispute,
2, 26–28, 58, 59
BMW, 39, 41
Boittin, Jean François, 18
Bovine somatotropin (BST) trade
dispute, 24–26, 58–59, 63
Brazil, 48–49, 50
Bureau of European Consumers'
Unions (BEUC), 16, 22–23

CAFE standards. *See* Corporate
average fuel economy (CAFE)
standards
Canada: agricultural biotechnology
trade disputes, 17, 21–22, 28;
environmental regulation trade
disputes, 45, 46, 48–49, 51;
imports of U.S. beef, 23; ozone
layer protection, 54;
pharmaceutical agreements with

U.S., 32; size of trade with U.S.,
62
Cargill, 27
Cassis de Dijon (1979), 6–7
Chemical safety regulations,
harmonization of, 3, 6, 7, 52–54,
56
Ciba, 27
Clinton administration, 28
Codex Alimentarius Commission,
6, 19, 20–21, 26
Commerce, U.S. Department of,
11, 12, 42
Committee for the Proprietary
Medicinal Products, 33–35
Committee on Food Additives and
Contaminants, 19
Committee on Residues of
Veterinary Drugs in Food, 19
Committee on Sanitary and
Phytosanitary Measures, 20–21
Confederation of European Paper
Industries (CEPI), 49
Congress, U.S., 40, 42, 54, 59
Convention on International Trade
in Endangered Species of Wild
Fauna and Flora (CITES), 7
Copenhagen amendments to
Montreal Protocols, 55–56
Corn, bioengineered, trade
dispute, 27. *See also*
Bioengineered crops trade
dispute
Corporate average fuel economy
(CAFE) standards, 61; GATT
dispute panel ruling, 2–3, 40–41;
impact on European
manufacturers, 38–40; U.S.
opposition, 58; U.S. support
groups, 59, 60, 63
Costa Rica, 42, 43
Council of Ministers, European
Union: ban on beef hormones,
15–17; beef hormone study, 15,
18, 21; regulatory policymaking

procedures, 9–10. *See also*
European Commission
Cresson, Edith, 18
Crops, bioengineered, trade
dispute, 2, 26–28, 58, 59

Decision of the Council Concerning
the Mutual Acceptance of Data
in the Assessment of Chemicals,
53–54
Denman, Roy, 18
Denmark, 16, 55
Directorate-General for External
Relations, 10
Dolphin protection efforts, 3, 41–
44, 59
Dunkel, Arthur, 20
Dunkel draft, Agreement on
Technical Barriers to Trade, 20
DuPont, 54

Earth Island Institute, 42
Eco-labeling trade dispute, 2;
European Commission
proposals, 47–48, 51; European
public support, 47, 59, 61;
nontariff trade barrier
perceptions, 48–52
Eizenstat, Stuart, 50
Eli Lilly, 25
Environmental activism, Europe:
impact on EU-U.S. trade
tensions, 59–60; ozone layer
protection, 55; wildlife
conservation, 44–45, 59, 63
Environmental Protection Agency,
U.S., 55
Environmental regulation: impact
on trade tensions, 51–52, 59–60,
63. *See also specific trade disputes*
Environment Policy Committee, 53
Equivalency principle, eco-labeling,
51
European Commission: beef
hormone trade dispute, 15, 21;
BST ban proposal, 24–25;

eco-label proposals, 47, 51; leg-hold trap ban trade dispute, 45–46; mutual recognition discussions with U.S., 8–9, 30, 32–33, 52–53; proposed labeling of bioengineered crops, 27–28
European Council, 26, 44–46, 52
European Court of Justice, 6–7, 65
European Medicines Evaluation Agency (EMEA), 32, 33–34, 36–37
European Parliament, 15, 27, 45
European Union-U.S. Interservice Group, 10

Fischler, Franz, 21, 22
Fleet accounting rules for CAFE, 41
Food and Drug Administration, U.S., 26, 32, 33–34, 36–37
Foreign direct investment, 8. *See also* Trade revenues and volumes, EU-U.S.
Fortress Europe, 8–9, 23. *See also* Single market, European
Framework Directive on Dangerous Substances (*1967*), 52–53
France: agriculture biotechnology trade disputes, 16, 22, 28; environmental regulation trade disputes, 42, 51; imports of U.S. beef, 17; ozone layer protection, 55; Panama Declaration, 43
Friends of the Earth, 40
Fuel economy standards trade dispute, 2–3, 38–41, 59, 60, 61, 63

Gas guzzler tax: GATT dispute panel ruling, 40–41; impact on European manufacturers, 38, 39, 40. *See also* Corporate average fuel economy (CAFE) standards
General Agreement on Tariffs and Trade (GATT), 2, 5, 7, 50; EU-U.S. automobile trade dispute, 3,

38–41; oversight of food safety regulations, 19–21; tuna embargo dispute, 2–3, 42–43. *See also* Agreement on Technical Barriers to Trade; World Trade Organization (WTO)
Genetically engineered crops trade dispute, 2, 26–28, 58, 59
Germany, 16, 51, 52, 55, 56
Glickman, Dan, 27–28
Gonal-F, 32
Great Britain, 16, 46, 51, 52, 55
Greece, 16

Harmonization of regulations, European Community/Union, 2; beef hormones, 16–17; impact on EU-U.S. regulatory cooperation, 8–11; leg-hold traps, 44–45; pharmaceutical products, 31–32; single-market objectives, 15–16, 17, 23, 28, 32, 59
Harmonization of regulations, international, 5–7; beef hormones, 19, 21, 64; chemical testing, 53–54; eco-labeling, 49–51; food safety, 20–21; impact of EU-U.S. cooperation, 1–2, 54, 64–66; importance, 3–5, 7, 56, 65–66; ozone layer protection, 55–56; pharmaceutical products, 6, 7, 33–35, 56, 62, 64; wild life conservation, 43, 45–46, 64. *See also* General Agreement on Tariffs and Trade (GATT); Regulatory cooperation; World Trade Organization (WTO)
Health and Welfare, Japan Ministry of, 33–34
High Seas Drift Fisheries Enforcement Act of *1992*, 44
Hills, Carla, 25
Hormones, growth. *See* Beef trade dispute; Bovine somatotropin (BST) trade dispute

ICI, 55

International Conference on Harmonization of Technical Requirements for the Registration of Pharmaceuticals for Human Use (ICH), 6, 7, 33–37, 56, 62, 64

International Electrotechnical Commission, 6

International Federation of Pharmaceutical Manufacturers Association, 33

International Organization for Standardization, 6

International Standardization Organization, 45–46, 51

Ireland, 16

Italy: agricultural biotechnology trade disputes, 16, 28; environmental regulation trade disputes, 42, 43, 44; ozone layer protection, 55; veal hormone crisis, 15

Jaguar, 39

Japan: cooperative regulation of pharmaceutical products, 7, 32, 33–35; imports of U.S. beef, 23; nontariff trade barriers, 20, 62; and U.S. automobile standards, 39; U.S. tuna embargo, 42

Kantor, Mickey, 41

Kessler, David, 34

Legal rulings, 6–7, 42

Leg-hold trap ban trade dispute, 2–3, 44–46, 51–52, 58, 59, 63, 64

Luxembourg, 28

Luxury car tax: GATT dispute panel ruling, 40–41; impact on European manufacturers, 38, 39–40. *See also* Corporate average fuel economy (CAFE) standards

Maastricht Treaty on European Union (*1992*), 31–32

MacSherry, Ray, 24–25

Maize, bioengineered, trade dispute, 27. *See also* Bioengineered crops trade dispute

Marine Mammal Protection Act (*1972*), 42

Meat inspection trade dispute, 2–3, 28–31

Mercedes-Benz, 39, 40, 41

Mexico, 23, 42, 43

Minimum data blueprint guideline (pharmaceuticals), 33–34

Monsanto, 25, 26, 27

Montreal Protocol, 7, 55–56, 64

Mosbacher, Robert, 9

Mutual recognition agreements (EU-U.S.): animal products inspection standards, 30–31; initiation of, 8–12; pharmaceutical products, 32–33, 36–37

Mutual recognition principle, 6–7, 51

Netherlands, 16, 46, 55

New Zealand, 20, 21–22

Norway, 54

Organization for Economic Cooperation and Development (OECD), 6, 7, 53–54, 62, 64

Ozone layer protection efforts, 3, 54–56

Panama, 42

Panama Declaration, 43

Pharmaceutical products, harmonization of regulations: EU-U.S, 3, 14–15, 31–33, 36–37; international, 6, 7, 33–35, 56, 62, 64

Pork ban trade dispute, 29–30. *See also* Meat inspection trade dispute

Portugal, 44

Poultry ban trade dispute, 30–31. *See also* Meat inspection trade dispute

President's Council on Competitiveness, 33

Proportionality principle, 5

Public opinion, European: agricultural biotechnology, 15–16, 18, 22–23, 26, 59, 61; eco-labeling, 47; pressures for regulation proposals, 59–60. *See also* Environmental regulation

Regulatory cooperation: business demands for, 8, 11–12, 55; importance, 3–5, 7, 65–66; obstacles, 1–2, 6, 9–10, 13, 14, 61–63. *See also* Harmonization of regulations, international

Regulatory redundancy, costs of, 4, 5, 12, 34

Russia, 46

Saab-Scania, 39

Scrivener, Christiance, 8

Shuman, A. B., 39

Single European Act (*1987*), 57–58

Single market, European: actions to support, 15–17, 28, 32, 44–45, 47–48; barriers to creating, 29, 31

Soviet Union, 45

Soybeans, bioengineered, trade dispute, 26–28. *See also* Bioengineered crops trade dispute

Spain, 43, 44

SPS Agreement (Agreement on Sanitary and Phytosanitary Measures), 20–21

Standard on Environmental Labels and Declaration (Draft Standard 14020), 51

Standards Code. *See* Agreement on Technical Barriers to Trade

Standing Veterinary Committee, 29

Sub-Cabinet Group, 10–11

Sullivan, Louis W., 33

Sweden, 32, 54

Switzerland, 32

Tariffs, retaliatory, 18–19, 21

Taxes, automobile: GATT dispute panel ruling, 3, 40–41; impact on European manufacturers, 38–40. *See also* Corporate average fuel economy (CAFE) standards

Test Guidelines (chemical), 53–54

Third Country Meat Directive (TCMD), 29–30

Toxic Substances Control Act of *1976* (TSCA), 52–53

Trade and Environment Committee, 49, 51–52

Trade disputes: impact of European single-market objectives, 2, 8–9, 23, 36, 52, 59–60; impact of public opinion, 13, 28, 59–62; lack of protectionist intent, 12–13, 58–59, 62, 63. *See also specific trade disputes*

Trade Representative, Office of the U.S., 29, 30, 48

Trade revenues and volumes, EU-U.S., 3, 8–9, 12, 62–63; agricultural products, 17, 18–19, 23, 25, 27, 30–31

Transatlantic Advisory Committee on Standards, Certification, and Regulatory Policy, 11

Transatlantic Business Dialogue (TABD) conferences, 11–12

Transatlantic Declaration of *1990*, 9

Tuna embargo trade dispute, 2–3, 41–43, 46, 51–52, 58, 59, 63

Unilever, 26

Unit for Regulatory Relations with the United States, 10

Upjohn, 25
Uruguay Round: establishment of
    mutual recognition principle, 6–
    7; harmonization of food safety
    regulations, 20–21; impact of EU-
    U.S. cooperation, 65;
    strengthening of proportionality
    principle, 5–6; and U.S.
    Congress, 40

Venezuela, 42, 43

Wildlife conservation trade
    disputes, 2–3, 51–52, 58; impact
    of environmental activists, 59,
    63; leg-hold traps, 44–46, 64;
    marine life, 41–44, 46, 60

Williams, Roger, 35
Working Group on Environmental
    Measures and International
    Trade, 49–50
World Health Organization, 35
World Trade Organization (WTO),
    2, 44, 64–65; beef hormone trade
    dispute, 3, 21–22; eco-labeling
    trade dispute, 49–51, 52;
    harmonization of regulations, 5–
    7, 14, 20–21. *See also* General
    Agreement on Tariffs and Trade
    (GATT)

Yeutter, Clayton, 20, 23–24, 25
Young, Frank, 23